# *Lichens*

## naturally scottish

© Scottish Natural Heritage 2004

ISBN 1 85397 373 4 paperback

A CIPO record is held at the British Library

W3K0304

**Acknowledgements:** Advice and comments from Sandy and Brian Coppins

**Author:** Oliver Gilbert

**Series Editor:** Lynne Farrell (SNH)

**Design and production:** SNH Design and Publications

Photographs:

**K. Dalby** 2, 3, 16, 19 (inset); **L.Farrell/SNH** 29; **B.Fox** 36; **A.Fryday** 24; **L. Gill/SNH** back cover top left, frontispiece, contents, opposite 1, 5 top left, 5 right, 5 bottom left, 9 top, 9 bottom, 13, 15, 17, 19, 20, 25, 27 28, 31, 33, 35 top left, 35 top right, 35 bottom; **P&A Macdonald/SNH** 23; **I. Munro** front cover, 1, 6 (inset); **J.Petrie/Inverness Museum and Art Gallery** 7; **G.Satterley** 6.

Illustrations:

**Bill Thompson** 11 left (adapted from map by A. E. G. Averis) & 11 right (source: Gilbert 1974);
**Dundee City Council, Museums and Art Galleries in conjunction with Dundee Naturalist Society** 12.

Scottish Natural Heritage

Design and Publications

Battleby

Redgorton

Perth PH1 3EW

Tel: 01738 458530

Fax: 01738 458613

E-mail: pubs@snh.gov.uk

www.snh.org.uk

**Cover photograph:**
Mountain saffron (*Solorina crocea*) - a rare alpine species found in the Scottish Highlands

**Frontispiece:**
Several species of lichen completely covering a rock

**Back Cover photograph:**
Blood-spot (*Ophioparma ventosum*) - a common lichen in mountain areas

# Lichens

## naturally scottish

by

Oliver Gilbert

# Foreword

Whilst Scotland's outstanding scenery is internationally renowned, the fact that its lichen communities are also of international importance is scarcely recognised. In commissioning this book from one of Britain's leading lichenologists, Scottish Natural Heritage is seeking to put that right.

Oliver Gilbert outlines their place in folklore and their role in the one-time world-famous Harris Tweed economy, but it is when he comes to describe some of the special places where lichens thrive that one senses just why these strange organisms make his spine tingle.

Those venturing onto the high ground of the Cairngorm plateau will find themselves in a lichen-dominated wilderness, which Oliver and his friend Brian Fox did much to describe. Some parts of the Celtic rain forest, their trees 'dripping' with lichens, are so remote they are still not fully explored for lichens, but you do not have to know the names of the lichens to know that you are somewhere special.

The importance of some habitats has only been recognised in recent years. It was not until the late 1970s that Brian Coppins of the Royal Botanic Garden Edinburgh realised that the twigs of Atlantic hazelwoods supported a distinctive lichen flora. One species discovered and named by him and Peter James of the Natural History Museum was the white-script lichen - probably endemic to Scotland.

Since Victorian times, lichens have been known to be good indicators of air pollution - rather like the canary down the coal mine. Back in those times, sulphur was the problem but this has largely been conquered with the clean air acts. Now the problems include nitrogen from both agriculture and vehicle exhausts, and global warming which may account for the apparent disappearance of certain species of snow-bed lichen in the Cairngorms. Global measures are required to conserve such lichen communities.

Lichens colour the landscape, especially where the air is 'pure as wine', but look closely at bark, wood and rock and you will see just how beautiful their intricate structures can be. Their fruit bodies, through which reproductive spores are produced, differ on the various species, some being like miniature jam tarts, others tiny volcanoes and, perhaps most fascinating of all - the 'writing' lichens - so called because of their resemblance to hieroglyphics.

Lichenology is a neglected science, but Oliver's account conveys the excitement of the chase.

*Stephen Ward*

Stephen Ward
Formerly Advisory Officer on Lichens,
Scottish Natural Heritage

Old Man's Beard *(Usnea sp.)* and Oak Moss *(Evernia prunastri)* growing on a birch tree by Loch Ness

# Contents

Lichen-covered oak trees at Ariundle National Nature Reserve (NNR), Ardnamurchan, Westerness

# Lichens in Scotland

Lichens are more abundant and better developed in Scotland than in other parts of the British Isles. Many people notice lichens for the first time as they see dense, shaggy coats on tree trunks and rocks - 'old man's beard' hangs to a foot long off branches. Spectacular patches of scarlet-tipped lichens are often found on heathland.   Those venturing onto the high ground of the Cairngorm plateau, will find themselves in a wilderness dominated by lichens.

In the past lichens played an important role in the Scottish economy.   They were used for dyeing, both on a domestic scale and in supplying the manufacturers of the world-famous Harris tweed with their shades from orange through to brown.   Even now you can bring back a jersey knitted with lichen-dyed wool as a memento of a visit to Scotland.   The only naturalised reindeer in Britain are found in the Highlands where they live for much of the year on the lichen known as 'reindeer moss'.

From the point of view of Scotland's natural heritage, many of the lichen communities in western Scotland are unequalled anywhere in Europe and so are of international importance.

Particularly Scottish are:

- the Celtic rain forests,
- Caledonian pinewoods,
- Atlantic hazelwoods,
- the lichens of the vast bird colonies on islands such as St Kilda,
- the montane communities are exceptional, where a single mountain can exceed in diversity the combined lichen floras of Snowdonia and the English Lake District.

This booklet provides an introduction to these riches.

Reindeer Moss *(Cladonia portentosa)*

1

Orange Sea Star *(Caloplaca verruculifera)* common on rocky shores

# What is a lichen?

A lichen (pronounced li'ken) is a dual organism consisting of a fungus and a photosynthetic alga or blue-green alga (cyanobaterium) which live in close association. The photosynthetic partner manufactures food for the whole lichen and the fungus provides a stable, protective environment for its alga. The fungus forms the main body of the lichen, and in most cases, the alga lies sandwiched between upper and lower fungal layers. Where a lichen has a green algal partner, the green algal layer can often be seen by scratching the upper surface of the lichen. Lichens are often quoted as a classic example of symbiosis - a mutually beneficial partnership between two organisms.

Other interesting facts:

- some crust-like lichens on rocks have a 'legendary slow' growth rate, sometimes as little as 0.1 mm per year,

- in undisturbed conditions, some rock-dwelling lichens can survive to a great age (many hundreds of years) and are among the oldest living organisms in Scotland,

- many lichens have a remarkable tolerance to drying out, during which state they can survive extremes of heat and cold; this means that they can tolerate being scorched by the sun in summer months, yet also survive ice and snow, and are therefore able to grow higher up in the mountains than other plants.

Scottish lichens are many colours: white, grey, black, yellow, orange, sulphur, apple-green, pink or scarlet. Most grow as crusts, some are leafy (foliose), while others are shrubby. They are completely different from the mosses and liverworts with which they often grow. The majority of mosses and liverworts are green, leafy and photosynthesise their own food.

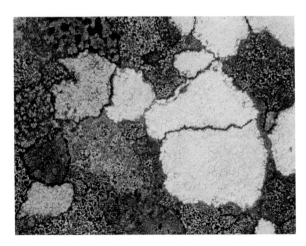

Slow-growing lichen (*Lecanora rupicola*), Shetland

3

# How lichens multiply and disperse

The upper surface of many lichens bears special structures which appear as miniature jam tarts, delicate cups, or tiny volcanoes with a minute pore at the tip. Some are brightly coloured, others more muted, and many are black.   A special group of crustose lichens found on the smooth bark of hazel, rowan, holly and ash (particularly in the west) are known as 'script lichens' as they have short, scribble-like lines scattered over their surface.   All these structures are known as 'fruit bodies' as they forcibly discharge tiny spores to a height of a few millimeters where they have a good chance of becoming airborne.

Reproduction by spores is a risky business as, on landing and germination, they need to meet the right algal partner before they can form a new lichen.

Many lichens increase their chance of successful reproduction by producing special parts that become detached and grow into a new plant (propagules) containing both alga and fungus.   The most common are powdery structures (soralia) that develop as pustules on the upper surface.   These release small clumps of algal cells (soredia) held together by a web of fungal threads (hyphae).   The other structures for vegetative reproduction, also unique to lichens, are isidia.   These are fragile, peg-like outgrowths on the upper surface which contain both partners.   Numerous lichen isidia and soredia are picked up following stormy nights by pollen-sampling equipment run for hay-fever sufferers in a rooftop location in Edinburgh

If you look through a hand lens you will see that the upper surfaces of lichens with their varied fruit bodies, soralia, isidia and range of hues look extremely beautiful.

4

Sea Ivory *(Ramalina siliquosa)*

A Dog Lichen *(Peltigera sp.)*

Script Lichen *(Graphis scripta)* growing on a rowan tree at the Birks of Aberfeldy

Inside a Harris tweed factory with some of the lichen-dyed wool
Inset: Cudbear *(Ochrolechia tartarea)*

# Use of lichens for dyeing

By far the most important use of lichens in Scotland was for dyeing, first as a cottage industry and later on a commercial scale. The lichens were scraped off the rocks using metal hoops, spoons and, in the poorer districts, seashells. Here is an account of lichen dyeing from Shetland records:

'My aunt was the one for making dyed yarn. I mind seeing her work with yon scrottyie, yon grey lichen you scrape from the stanes. She made up a brawly thick gruel, ye ken, and had it boiling abun the fire in a muckle three-taed kettle, with layers of yarn packed between. A few hanks came out soon and the rest she'd leave a while longer to get a darker shade. She'd knit her stockings striped in different shades of brown'.
Venables 1956, Life in Shetland: a world apart

As late as the 1950s, black, three-legged iron pots used for boiling lichens could be seen outside many crofts in the Hebrides. The browns and fawns of Harris tweed were produced from a closely-related group of lichens called crottle. The last of a long line of commercial dyers and hand weavers of this cloth on Harris ceased production in 1997.

The other main lichen dye produced in Scotland and, exported all over Britain, was orchil or cudbear, which gave a coveted purple or red. Its commercial value was so great that a factory producing this household dye was set up in Glasgow covering 17 acres and processing 250 tons of lichen each year. Gathering the lichen provided considerable employment in the Highlands. This gave rise to the Scottish saying:

'Cattle on the hills, Gold on the stones.'

Three-legged iron pot used for boiling lichens

7

# What's in a name?

Many Scottish lichens have three names:

- a Gaelic name, once regularly used by the Highlanders and Islanders, but now forgotten and only found in dictionaries. They used crottle as a general term for lichens,

- a Common name which refers to some conspicuous feature or property. Two of the examples given have old names, dating back to Mediaeval times, when physicians practised a 'Doctrine of Signatures'. They believed that parts of the plants that bore some resemblance to parts of the human anatomy had special properties to heal ailments occurring in the affected parts of the human body. Anyone with a lung complaint, for example, would be made a concoction of lungwort,

- the scientific Latin name which is also descriptive of the species if you are a classical scholar.

The Common names of many Scottish lichens are pure poetry: Sunburn, Rock Hair, Yellow Candles, Golden Pine Lichen, Little Clouds, Oak Moss, Crab's-eye, Coral Crust and Sea Ivory.

**Gaelic:** Crotal Coille - wood crottle,

**Common:** Tree Lungwort - due to the underside of its lobes bearing a resemblance to the inside of a lung,

**Latin:** *Lobaria pulmonaria*

**Gaelic:** Lus Ghoinnich - a plant for wounds,

**Common:** Dog Lichen - a cure for the bite of a mad dog - due to the underside bearing fang-like structures,

**Latin:** *Peltigera canina*

**Gaelic:** Crotal Dubh - dark crottle,

**Common:** Heather-rags - ragged and grey, growing amongst the heather,

**Latin:** *Hypogymnia physodes*

Tree Lungwort *(Lobaria pulmonaria)* on an oak tree near Arisaig

Heather-rags *(Hypogymnia physodes)* growing on a blanket bog in North Uist

# The exceptional Scottish climate

Lying on the western seaboard of Europe, in the track of the Atlantic depressions, Scotland has a climate that is unique in Europe. It is described as extreme oceanic i.e. it is influenced by the surrounding seas. The diagram opposite shows how even the Scandinavian fjords, Brittany, Cornwall and Wales have lower oceanicity scores. High values indicate a combination of extreme humidity, abundant rainfall and number of rain days (days when rain falls), persistent cloudiness, cool summers and mild winters. The Gulf Stream helps to make the climate warmer with the result that along the west coast there are numerous sites, such as Inverewe Gardens, where palm trees flourish.

Woodland lichens which grow best in, or require, a mild, wet climate thrive here. Oak woods bordering the western sea lochs are 'dripping' with lichens that are rare in Europe as a whole.

A number of these lichens are endemic to Scotland which means they occur nowhere else in the world.

The unusual climate affects all lichen communities. The mountains in the west experience a lower snow cover than those elsewhere and their rocks are so continuously wet that lichen species normally restricted to damp rock are ubiquitous. The wet ground favours peat formation so some flat areas are covered with a community known as blanket bog. The sodden moorland that results has its own suite of very beautiful lichens which can be seen beside trackways or around the margins of disused peat cuttings. These include clumps of reindeer lichens, patches of pixie-cup and horn lichens (*Cladonia* species).

## Map showing the gradient of oceanicity across Europe

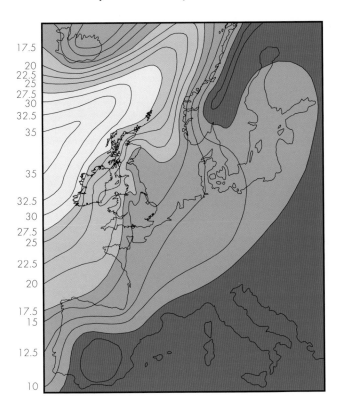

## Mucky Air Map - produced by school children, showing the polluted and cleaner air over Britain

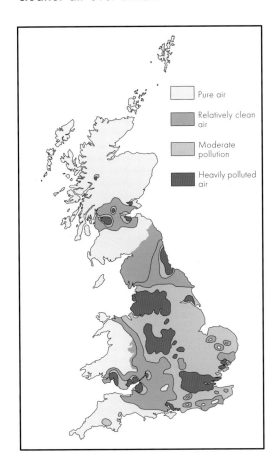

Pure air

Relatively clean air

Moderate pollution

Heavily polluted air

# Air as pure as wine?

Most people are aware that lichens do not grow well where there is air pollution. They are like the canary down the coal mine - detecting air pollution at lower levels than many other organisms. In 1972 school children throughout Britain mapped lichens around their homes which helped produce the 'Mucky air map of Britain'. It revealed that the largest reservoirs of pure air are in Scotland, which, apart from Scotland's Midland Valley, appears to enjoy air as pure as wine. This is not quite the full story however.

The school children's map reflected the distribution of sulphur dioxide to which virtually all lichens are sensitive. However there are several different types of air pollution. Despite a big drop in sulphur dioxide levels, acid rain which travels a lot further, is still affecting certain woodland lichens - for instance along the southern edge of the Highlands and the remoter areas of the Cowal peninsula. In addition, residents in the Cairngorms have reported up to five centimetres of highly-acidic, black snow falling several times a year. When it melts this produces a pulse of toxic water, but its effect on lichens is not known. A further cause of concern is increasing long-distance nitrogen pollution from sources associated with industry, transport and agriculture.

This goes to show that we must not be complacent about air pollution effects on Scottish lichens and assume that remoteness from sources will always protect them. But for the time being, areas north of the Highland Boundary Fault enjoy some of the cleanest air in Europe.

**Sulphur dioxide levels around Dundee in 1976**

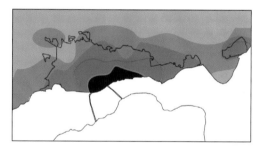

**Sulphur dioxide levels around Dundee in 2000**

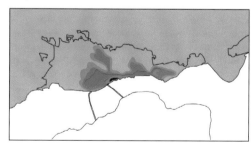

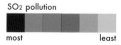

SO2 pollution

most          least

12

*Sticta limbata* is particularly sensitive to acid rain but is still widespread in the woodlands of western Scotland

# Important habitats for lichens

## The Celtic rain forest

The west of Scotland holds very wet and mossy, oak and hazel woods which are internationally important for their lichens, mosses and liverworts. Their higher plant flora is not particularly special. It is the epiphytes (plants which grow on other plants without being parasitic) clothing the trees that are exceptional. The woods are best developed along the sides of sheltered sea lochs such as Sunart, Shiel and Moidart. Some of these woods are so remote that they still have not been fully explored for lichens.

It is quite an experience to visit these Celtic rain forests. The trees are of only a moderate size and the first impression is of how mossy the habitat is - a deep blanket of moss covers the floor, climbs the tree trunks, festoons horizontal boughs, and even extends into the canopy. By absorbing rain and mist, then releasing this moisture slowly, the blanket of mosses and liverworts helps maintain the very high humidity. The moss forms the base on which the rare lichen communities are found, especially one called the 'Lobarion' after its most conspicuous family. There are four species of lungworts *(Lobaria)* that can grow to the size of dinner plates. Growing with these are lead-grey *Pannaria*, *Parmeliella* and *Degelia* species, dark *Stictas* and jelly lichens, *Biatora sphaeroides* with pink fruits and *Dimerella lutea* with bright yellow ones. The trees often have a skirt of dog lichen *(Peltigera)* which has abundant shield-like, chestnut-coloured fruit bodies. The weight of the lichen cover eventually becomes so great that the moss peels off the trees, leaving heaps of these internationally rare lichens around their base.

You do not have to know the names of the lichens to realise that you are somewhere very special.

Veteran oak tree covered in lichens, mosses and ferns, Ariundle NNR, Ardnamurchan

The best lichen sites are on sunny, south-facing slopes while the rare Atlantic mosses and liverworts, which need more moisture, favour northern aspects. The optimal sites for lichens are also well lit being around the edge of glades or along woodland margins.

While the whole area is a lichenologists' Mecca, sites where burns and gorges cut through the woodland are particularly special. Here, in ravines full of tangled vegetation, there is a wider range of trees - oak together with ash, elm, cherry and willows. Ash and hazel have a more alkaline bark and are a home to 'jewels' such as the handsome Specklebellies (*Pseudocyphellaria* species) and Blackberries and Custard *(Parmentaria chilense)*.

On higher ground the oak woods give way to grazed birch woodland which is a different, but equally distinctive, lichen-rich variant of Celtic rain forest. It is dominated by silvery-grey leafy species many of which grow directly on tree bark. This bark has a high acidity due to 'washing out' or leaching by the high rainfall.

These western woods are far from being undisturbed relics of the ancient forest. In times past, these woods were extensively coppiced, and the wood used for charcoal, tanning and bobbin-making. This activity ceased about 150 years ago, but it is thought there was always sufficient wildwood remaining for the entire suite of rare lichens to survive. Today the best examples of these woodlands are managed for nature conservation.

Netted Shield Lichen *(Parmelia sulcata)* showing the powdery reproductive parts *(soralia)*

Golden-edged Specklebelly *(Pseudocyphellaria crocata)* growing at Ballachuan hazelwood, Argyll

# Caledonian pinewoods

It is a myth that the Scottish Highlands were once covered by a vast pine wood called 'The Great Wood of Caledon'. Pollen analysis tells us that pine has always been patchily distributed. The native pinewoods are the surviving fragments of the ancient Caledonian pine forests. Today pinewoods cover an area of around only 10,000 hectares. Some of their strongholds are Glen Affric, the Black Wood of Rannoch, Rothiemurchus, and hill slopes beside Loch Maree. The woods are composed of Scots pine *Pinus sylvatica* subspecies *scotica*. This is restricted to Scotland, has short needles and maintains a pyramidal form until late in life when it becomes round-headed.

These woods have so far yielded more than 430 epiphytic lichens of which 222 have been found on pine. The rest are on associated rowan, birch and juniper. Seventeen of these lichens are found nowhere else in the British Isles so this is another particularly Scottish community.

Lichen cover is most often best developed on ancient 'granny pines', in sheltered situations. Here the bark plates are welded together by thick, multi-coloured lichen crusts, scrambling leaf-like species and festoons of yellow-grey *Usnea* and horse-hair brown *Bryoria*. The rare Witches' Hair *(Alectoria sarmentosa)* occurs in spectacular swathes on the lower branches of pine in valleys in the west.

A major difference from deciduous forests is that a high proportion of the lichens are found on stumps and standing dead trees. This habitat may be very sparse, less than one tree per hectare, but is of the utmost importance as slowly decaying pines that have lost their bark hold many of the pinewood specialities. These standing pillars of dead wood, and recently fallen ones, are picturesquely known as the 'bones of the forest'. Pinhead lichens looking exactly like their name, often form swards on sheltered parts of the 'bones'. Being small it is often easiest to locate them by manoeuvring so that a patch of bark is seen against the sky. If present, they can be seen in silhouette. Up to eight types of Pinhead lichen may be present and can be distinguished by their colours - green, yellow, rusty, grey, black or brown.

Pinewood, Glen Affric. Many of the lichens here are epiphytic -
growing on another plant without being parasitic
Inset: Pinhead lichen *(Chaenotheca brunneola)*

Hazel stems covered in mosses, liverworts and crustose lichens

# Atlantic hazelwoods

Hazel forms a lower storey in oak woods or is a hedgerow shrub growing throughout most of Britain. In the west of Scotland, however, it forms pure woods on steep slopes facing the sea. Hazelwoods have probably occupied these sites for 9,000 years, the extreme exposure preventing invasion and over-topping by other trees. Hazel enjoys the benefit of being able to persist indefinitely under grazing and has a partiality for soils developed over basalt that are widespread along the coast around Oban and on the islands of Mull, Eigg and Skye.

The lichen interest of these pure hazelwoods only started to be recognised in the late 1970s when Brian Coppins, lichenologist at the Royal Botanic Garden, Edinburgh, realised that they contained many distinctive species, some new to Britain, others new to science. An example is the White Script lichen *(Graphis alboscripta)* which has so far not been found outside this habitat and is regarded as a Scottish endemic.

On entering a hazelwood the 'brush' of thin stems that make up a high proportion of each individual can be seen to be covered with a dense, pale, mosaic of small lichens which give the bark a silvery hue. These can be distinguished by subtle shades of colour and the small dots, scribbles and tiny 'volcanic craters' through which their spores are ejected.

High-quality, old-growth hazelwoods contain trunks of all sizes including very large individuals with rough moss-covered bark which are around 70-100 years old. These support a very different range of lichens to those found on the smooth thin stems. Here large leafy species of the 'Lobarion' are dominant. Despite the woods having the appearance of a past history of coppice management this is not the case. On Eigg, Cleadale Woods were last exploited during the 1940s when a wartime coal shortage led the crofters to cut the larger stems for firewood.

The best season to explore this unique habitat is late spring, before the interior becomes shaded by the expanding leaves. At this time the woods are bright with primroses, violets and bluebells, sunlight filters through the branches, and birdsong is at its height. To investigate a lichen flora of international importance against this background is magical and a particularly Scottish experience.

21

# Alpines galore

Only a tiny fraction of Scotland is over 914 metres high (or 3,000 feet if you are a Munroist) but this small area, above the upper limit of heather, is home to a vegetation dominated by lichen, moss and sedge heath. This is the nearest we have to tundra in Britain. The Scottish montane lichen flora comprises about 400 species and includes nearly a third (52) of the British Red List lichens so it is very special (see p34). It is possible to walk all day in the hills and encounter only common upland species. The rarities have particular habitat requirements that need to be appreciated and some of these are outlined.

The Cairngorm Plateau is the place to study lichens associated with late snow patches. These species are left-overs from the last Ice Age. The largest patches are almost permanent, melting on average once every 25 years. The lichens are concentrically-zoned around them depending on their tolerance to snow lie; the inner-most ones can survive years of burial. Ice-cold melt-water streams issuing from the toe of the snow patches are also good lichen-hunting grounds. Lichens form a skin over the soft ground or occur on the moss cushions covering small boulders. The handsome, green *Lecanora leptacina* is absolutely restricted to these sites. Recently moss cushions were found supporting an undescribed

lichen with tiny reddish fruits and the discoverer, Alan Fryday named it in honour of his young daughter, Amelia.

A curious factor, which restricts the abundance of lichens on the granite boulders that litter the summit plateau, is abrasion from windblown gravel and needle-like ice crystals which blast and erode during winter blizzards. Several of the rarest lichens of this high 'tundra' have not been seen for over 20 years and are suspected of being casualties of global warming.

In contrast, Ben Nevis in the damper, milder west, supports a somewhat different alpine lichen flora. A species more common here than elsewhere is *Catolechia wahlenbergii*. This elegant lichen forms vivid yellow rosettes in dark crevices. It is protected under Schedule 8 of the Wildlife and Countryside Act 1981, as amended, and therefore has been given an English name. After some discussion it was named 'Goblin lights'.

As Ben Nevis is the highest point in Britain it was hoped that a recent survey of the summit area would produce at least one special lichen. We were not disappointed and in 1990 the first UK record of the suitably named *Staurothele arctica* was made a few yards from the summit cairn.

Aerial view of Ben Nevis, Britain's highest mountain at 1344 metres

The rare Goblin Lights *(Catolechia wahlenbergii)* found on Ben Nevis

A feature of these western hills that sets them apart from those in the east is that lichens which grow on the ground are rare. Instead, carpets of the Woolly Hair Moss *(Racomitrium lanuginosum)* form an undulating mattress over the ground. The distinctive lichens of the western Highlands mostly grow on rock.

The mountains considered so far have all been acid, which is the norm for the Highlands. But the foremost areas for arctic-alpines, flowering plants, mosses, and lichens alike, are those where calcareous rocks occur. The outstanding locality for this feature is the Breadalbane range in Perthshire. Here extensive deposits of soft, calcareous schist outcrop over a distance of 11.2 kilometres reaching a height of 1219 metres at one point. For two centuries botanists have been making pilgrimages to this area and, though the higher plants are now well-known, the lichens, which are twice as abundant, are still being investigated.

Calcareous outcrops on these mountains are restricted and often stumbled on by chance. But once such a site has been located it pays to spend several hours with hand lens and kneeling mat examining every 'square inch' of its surface. The rewards are great, ledges are crowded with rare and beautiful species that scramble over rock, soil, dead vegetation and moss. The communities are reminiscent of a minature rock garden and they have probably been growing undisturbed since the end of the Ice Age.

It is not just the outcrops that hold arctic-alpine lichens. The lichens extend into burns, lochans, summit grasslands and bare, gravelly areas. There is a lifetime of investigation to be undertaken. It is every lichenologist's dream to discover a new 'Ben Lawers'. Just one such area has come to light in recent decades - 40 kilometres away in the remote Ben Alder range.

Snow patches in Lurchers Gully and
Coire an Lochan, Cairngorms

# The coast

Several features combine to make the Scottish coast of special interest to lichenologists. The bird islands of St Kilda, North Rona and the Flannans; the machair; and the vast, east coast sand dunes deserve special mention.

The lichens produce distinct colour bands on coastal rocks:

- A black zone at sea level, above that,
- an orange zone heavily influenced by salt spray, and then,
- an upper, grey zone which is richest in lichens.

## Sea bird cities

Beyond the Outer Hebrides lies an arc of small remote islands known as the Furthest Hebrides. The islands are lapped by the waters of the Arctic Ocean, so sea temperatures remain low even in summer. These islands are home to millions of seabirds, their nests line the cliffs, the air is full of their cries, and they perch on every rock covering them with their droppings. It is these guano-spattered boulders that are special for the lichens. Each can support up to 25 species including such rarities as the golden-coloured *Caloplaca scopularis*, the brown *Amandinea coniops* and the sulphur-tinted *Lecanora straminea*. This is the main British habitat for these three species.

Around these remote, storm-lashed islands the coloured bands are uplifted so the black zone on the west coast of North Rona extends vertically to 16 metres above sea level, compared with a sheltered shore on the mainland, where it might be only one metre deep.

A typical lichen of the grey zone is Sea Ivory *Ramalina siliquosa* which forms dense shaggy swards in places exposed to the wind. On St Kilda, the agile Soay sheep supplement their diet by grazing on these swards during winter.

## Machair

Machair is a habitat unique to the west coasts of Scotland and Ireland. It develops where calcareous shell-sand blows inland converting the wet, acid, peaty landscape into a well-drained, flowery pasture. It is a feature of the west coast of the Inner and Outer Hebrides with islands such as Coll, Tiree, South Uist and Harris supporting the finest examples.

Lichen-covered boulders showing the zonation on the shore at Loch Sween, Taynish NNR

Lichen heath in the stabilized dunes at Tentsmuir NNR

The short, species-rich turf is sufficiently open to support a lichen community that has many species in common with chalk grassland. The richest sites are associated with low, partially sand-covered outcrops where crevice-loving species such as the socket lichens *(Solorina saccata, S.spongiosa)* and the apple-green Thrushwort *(Peltigera leucophlebia)* can find a foothold. Early summer is the time to explore the machair. The flowers are out, blue butterflies are on the wing, white surf lines the shore and the lichens - well, who knows what you will find?

## East coast dunes

Sandy beaches backed by dunes are a characteristic feature of Scotland's maritime scenery. The largest of these are on the east coast at Culbin, Forvie and Tentsmuir. These vast, remote dunes are exciting places where the lack of grazing, trampling and fire has resulted in the lichen swards developing an unusual luxuriance. Reindeer lichens, for example, form a deep, extensive white carpet spreading into the conifers planted many years ago, and suppressing all other growth.

Over 30 species of the lichen genus *Cladonia* have been recorded at Culbin, including a northern element better represented here than anywhere else in Britain.

A number of the ground-dwelling lichens, favoured by disturbance, are found along the edge of forestry tracks.

At Cuthill Links, on the north side of the Dornoch Firth, the lichen interest is concentrated on sandy valley floors separated by gorse-covered dune ridges. Here is the best place to go to see the curious phenomenon whereby normally alpine species descend to sea-level in the far north of Scotland. Lichens typical of mountain summits, such as *Thamnolia vermicularis*, which looks like a cluster of white worms, are found here. They grow luxuriantly on the sand within sight and sound of the sea. These east coast dune lichen communities have links with those on the Danish coast.

Heather and lichen heath at Cuthill Links, near Dornoch Firth - an internationally important site

# Blanket bog

Most level ground in the west of Scotland is naturally covered with a deep layer of peat, known as blanket bog. The surface vegetation, a mixture of Bog Moss (*Sphagnum*), various types of heather and cotton-grass, is very wet - too wet for most lichens. Lichens find an opening, however, where there has been disturbance perhaps associated with peat cutting, drainage or fire. Drier faces, ridges and baulks of peat are rapidly colonised by a range of attractive species. Particularly noticeable are a suite of red-fruited *Cladonia* species with common names such as Scarlet cups, British soldiers or Bengal matches. Others have brown fruits and are branched like deer's antlers, coral, or have fantastic 'Disney-world' shapes. Another series, the cup-lichens, again *Cladonia* species, have fruit bodies resembling trumpets or goblets.

These moorland lichens have attracted the attention of poets. Wordsworth wrote of them:

'Ah me what lovely tints are these,
Of olive, green, and scarlet bright!
In spikes and branches and in stars,
Green, red, and partly white.'

Though *Cladonia* species are dominant, and the first to attract attention, others are equally attractive. Very wet peat is the habitat of *Pycnothelia papillaria*, the thallus (plant body) of which has been compared to babies' molar teeth, and it is always a thrill to come across the large coral-pink fruits of the Heath Lichen (*Icmadophila ericetorum*).

Scarlet-cup Lichen *(Cladonia coccifera)* growing on a peat bog, Rannoch Moor

# Conservation

It should be clear by now that a number of lichen habitats in Scotland are of international importance, being richer and more extensively developed than anywhere else in Europe.

Happily, past threats from air pollution, inappropriate forestry, and sheer ignorance are receding fast. Unfortunately a new threat, global warming, is beyond the capability of national conservation bodies to counter and may already be responsible for the recent extinction of four high-alpine lichens, *Bellemerea alpina, Brodoa intestiniformis,* Snow Caloplaca *(Caloplaca nivalis),* Alpine Moss Pertusaria *(Pertusaria bryontha)* and the decline of several others.

Nitrogen pollution arising from industry, agriculture and transport is increasingly causing concern. Vigilance is still required at a site level with regard to potentially damaging operations and changes.

Examples of this are:

- hydroelectric schemes,
- ski development,
- road projects,
- the spread of rhododendron,
- lack of continuity of veteran trees, and
- the decline of wayside trees.

The promotion of lichen conservation in Scotland is shared by a number of organisations which keep in close contact despite lichenologists being thin on the ground. Most major threats get identified and their effects mitigated.

The British Lichen Society recruits amateur and professional lichenologists, helps train them through courses, and holds field meetings to explore little-known areas. It has an active Conservation Committee, and provides generally stimulating conditions for those wishing to pursue the study of lichens.

The Royal Botanic Garden Edinburgh provides advice through its resident lichenologist, at present Dr Brian Coppins. Preserved specimens of most of Scotland's lichens can be seen in the herbarium there. These provide a source of reference for both historical and modern records, and can help in identification work.

Lichen carpet at Culbin Forest, Moray

# Biodiversity Action Plan and the Red Data List

In 1996 a Red Data Book of Lichens in Britain was published. It contained descriptions of 208 of Britain's rarest lichens. Each of these lichens was placed in one of the following four internationally recognised threat categories: Extinct (29), Critically Endangered (27), Endangered (30), Vulnerable (91) and Rare (31). Many are montane calcicoles but even more occur in sheltered valley woodland along the west coast where the combination of a high rainfall, cool summers and mild winters favours the development of communities rich in spectacular genera containing blue-green algae.

To promote the conservation of 40 of the most important lichens, Scottish Natural Heritage funded in-depth studies that involved the production of Biological Action Plans or Species Dossiers. These comprised a review of the literature, herbarium searches, and intensive fieldwork. The results were often surprising - certain species turned out to be more widespread than expected, for example, Stump Lichen *(Cladonia botrytes, Gyalideopsis scotica)* while others were in steep decline *(Bacidia incompta, Cladonia peziziformis)*. When deciding on conservation priorities there is a difficulty. Should resources be directed towards saving species on the verge of extinction or are these at the edge of their range and unlikely to respond to conservation measures? It is probably wisest to concentrate on Scottish endemic species, the White Script Lichen *Graphis alboscripta* and *Halecania rhypodiza,* or those such as Norwegian Specklebelly *(Pseudocyphellaria norvegica)* for which Scotland is its European stronghold.

White Script Lichen *(Graphis alboscripta)*

Stump Lichen *(Cladonia botrytes)*

Norwegian Specklebelly *(Pseudocyphellaria norvegica)*

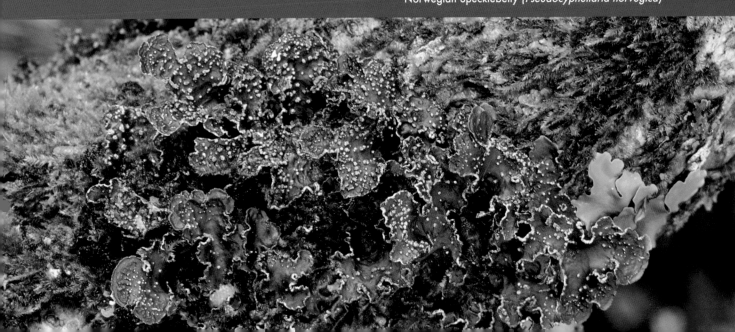

# Finding out more about lichens

Listed here are some starting points for anyone who wishes to learn more about lichens. Some of the books are on identification, others cover ecology, general biology, and uses of the lichens. Most people with a serious interest join the British Lichen Society or attend a course at a field centre.

Lichenologists at work on a fallen pine trunk

## Identification

Dalby, C. 1981 and 1987. *Lichens and Air Pollution* and *Lichens on Rocky Seashores.* British Museum (Natural History) and BP Educational Service.

Dobson, F.S. 2000. *Lichens: An illustrated guide to British and Irish species.* Richmond Publishing Co. Ltd., London. (Improvers).

Orange, A. 1994. *Lichens on Trees: a guide to some common species* National Museum of Wales, Cardiff. (Beginners).

Purvis, O.W, Coppins, B.J, Hawksworth, D.L, James, P.W, & Moore, D.M. 1992. *The Lichen Flora of Great Britain and Ireland.* Natural History Museum Publications with the British Lichen Society (the standard flora, in the process of being revised).

## Conservation

Church, J.M, Coppins, B.J, Gilbert, O.L, James, P.W, & Stewart, N.F. 1996. *Red Data Books of Britain and Ireland: lichens. Volume 1: Britain.* Joint Nature Conservation Committee, Peterborough.

Woods, R.G, & Coppins, B. J. 2003. *A Conservation Evaluation of British Lichens.* Natural History Museum Publications with the British Lichen Society.

## General aspects

Gilbert, O. 2000. *Lichens.* Collins New Naturalist Series, HarperCollins. (Covers all aspects of British lichens)

Purvis, W. 2000. *Lichens.* The Natural History Museum, London. (A popular guide to lichens world-wide).

Richardson, D. 1975. *The Vanishing Lichens.* David and Charles, Devon. (An account of their history, biology and importance; out of print).

## Useful Addresses

British Lichen Society, c/o Department of Botany, The Natural History Museum, Cromwell Road, London, SW7 5BD www.thebls.org.uk

Kindrogan Field Centre, Field Studies Council, Enochdhu, Blairgowrie, Perthshire, PH10 7PG Email: kindrogan@btinternet.com www.econet.org.uk/kindrogan

The Royal Botanic Garden, 20a Inverleith Row, Edinburgh, EH3 5LR. www.rbge.org.uk

## Also in the Naturally Scottish series...

If you have enjoyed Lichens why not find out more about Scotland's wildlife in our Naturally Scottish series. Each booklet looks at one or more of Scotland's native species. The clear and informative text is illustrated with exceptional photographs by top wildlife photographers, showing the species in their native habitats and illustrating their relationships with man. They also provide information on conservation and the law.

### Bumblebees

Did you know that Bummiebee, Droner and Foggie-toddler are all Scottish names for the bumblebee? Find out what these names mean and why bumblebees are so special inside this beautifully illustrated booklet. Also discover how you can help the bumblebee by planting appropriate flowers for their continued survival.
Murdo Macdonald
ISBN 1 85397 364 5 pbk 40pp £4.95

### Burnet Moths

Unlike many other species of moth, burnet moths fly by day. They can be easily recognised by their beautiful, glossy black wings with crimson spots. Their striking colouring is a very real warning to predators.
Mark Young
ISBN 1 85397 209 6 pbk 24pp £3.00

### Corncrakes

Secretive, skulking, rasping, loud, tuneless, scarce. . . all these words have been used to describe the corncrake. But once you could have added plentiful and widespread to the list. Now only a few birds visit Scotland each year. This booklet brings you the latest information on the corncrake and reveals this elusive and noisy bird in its grassy home.
ISBN  1 85397 049 2 pbk 40pp £3.95

### Fungi

Fungi belong to one of the most varied, useful and ancient kingdoms in the natural world. Scotland may have almost 2000 larger species with some of the most interesting found in our woodlands and grasslands. This booklet provides an introduction to their life cycles, habitats and conservation. Discover the fascinating forms of earthstars, truffles and waxcaps.
Roy Watling MBE and Stephen Ward
ISBN 1 85397 341 6 pbk 40pp £4.95

### Red Kites

This graceful and distinctive bird was absent from Scotland's skies for more than a century. Now with the help of a successful programme of re-introduction, it's russet plumage and forked tail can once again be seen in Scotland.
David Minns and Doug Gilbert
ISBN 1 85397 210 X pbk 24pp £3.95

### Red Squirrels

The red squirrel is one Scotland's most endearing mammals. This booklet provides an insight into their ecology and some of the problems facing red squirrels in Scotland today.
Peter Lurz & Mairi Cooper
ISBN 1 85397 298 4 pbk 20pp £3.00

### River Runners

Scotland's clean, cascading rivers contain a fascinating array of species. The atlantic salmon is the best known of our riverine species but others, such as lampreys and freshwater pearl mussels, are frequently overlooked but no less captivating. This booklet aims to illuminate aspects of their intriguing and largely unseen lifecycles, habitats and

conservation measures.
Iain Sime
ISBN 1 85397 353 X  pbk 44pp  £4.95

### Sea Eagles

This magnificent bird, with its wing span of over 2m is the largest bird of prey in Britain. In 1916 they became extinct, but a reintroduction programme began in 1975. This booklet documents the return of this truly majestic eagle. Production subsidised by Anheuser-Busch.
Greg Mudge, Kevin Duffy, Kate Thompson & John Love
ISBN 1 85397 208 8 pbk 16pp £1.50

# SNH Publications Order Form:
## Naturally Scottish Series

| Title | Price | Quantity |
|-------|-------|----------|
| Bumblebees | £4.95 | |
| Burnet Moths | £3.00 | |
| Corncrakes | £3.95 | |
| Fungi | £4.95 | |
| Lichens | £4.95 | |
| Red Kites | £3.95 | |
| Red Squirrels | £3.00 | |
| River Runners | £4.95 | |
| Sea Eagles | £1.50 | |

**Postage and packing:** free of charge in the UK, a standard charge of £2.95 will be applied to all orders from the European Union. Elsewhere a standard charge of £5.50 will be applied for postage.

Please complete in BLOCK CAPITALS

Name _____

Address _____

_____

_____

Post Code

Type of Credit Card   VISA ☐      MasterCard ☐

Name of card holder _____

Card Number

☐☐☐☐  ☐☐☐☐  ☐☐☐☐  ☐☐☐☐

Expiry Date  ☐☐ ☐☐

Send order and cheque made payable to Scottish Natural Heritage to:

Scottish Natural Heritage, Design and Publications, Battleby, Redgorton, Perth PH1 3EW

pubs@redgore.demon.co.uk

www.snh.org.uk

Please add my name to the mailing list for the:  SNH Magazine ☐

Publications Catalogue ☐

# AYURVEDA

# AYURVEDA

## FOR **HEALTH** AND **WELL-BEING**

**sally morningstar**

HOUSE
HERMES

**THIS BOOK IS FONDLY DEDICATED TO MY FIRST TEACHER - JOHN GARRIE ROSHI - AND TO ALL TEACHERS AND TEACHINGS THAT GUIDE US IN THE WAYS OF ANCIENT WISDOM.**

This Paperback edition published by
Hermes House

Hermes House is an imprint of Anness Publishing Limited
Hermes House, 88-89 Blackfriars Road, London SE1 8HA
tel. 020 7401 2077;  fax 020 7633 9499;  info@anness.com

A CIP catalogue record for this book is available from the British Library

ISBN 1 84081 479 9

Publisher: Joanna Lorenz
Project Editor: Sarah Duffin
Designer: Nigel Partridge
Photographer: Don Last
Illustrator: Anna Koska
Editorial Reader: Hayley Kerr

Printed and bound in China

1 3 5 7 9 10 8 6 4 2

MEDICAL DISCLAIMER
This book is an introductory guide to Ayuvedic Medicine and should in no way be used in
place of proper medical care. On no account should you receive treatment involving enemas, emesis or fasting from anyone other than a qualified practitioner. Consult your physician with any medical concerns.

# CONTENTS

# AYURVEDIC PRINCIPLES

AYURVEDA IS ACKNOWLEDGED AS THE traditional healing system of India, covering all aspects of life and lifestyle. Thousands of years old, it has influenced many other healing systems around the world. It was already established before the births of Buddha and Christ, and some biblical stories reflect the wisdom of Ayurvedic teachings.

There are many different branches to Ayurveda because it covers so many aspects of health and healing. These have been touched upon in this guide but the main emphasis is on dietary and lifestyle advice, specifically tailored to living in the Western world.

Ayurvedic medicine is founded on the belief that all diseases stem from the digestive system and are caused either by poor digestion of food, which is the body's major source of nourishment, or by following an improper diet for your *dosha* (nature). The system therefore concentrates to a large extent upon nutrition. There are three main humours (characteristics) or doshas – *vata* (ether and wind), *pitta* (fire and water) and *kapha* (water and earth) – and in this book you will find basic advice about suitable diets for the different doshas, as well as information about supportive treatments, including massage, exercise, colour, crystals, herbs and spices. There is also a tonic drink for each doshic type, and a list of common ailments that can be treated very effectively.

The following basic Ayurvedic approach will help you to develop some simple ways to keep yourself balanced in these days of increasing pressure, worry and stress. Identify your dosha, learn how to eat and live in accordance with your true nature, and discover how you can begin to heal your *vikruti* (current emotional, physical or mental health conditions) with the use of certain basic Ayurvedic methods.

*Dosha* means "that which tends to go out of balance easily". The elements, the seasons, your astrological chart, your genetic inheritance from your parents and environmental factors: all of these contribute to the potential for imbalance within the doshas. Ayurveda's philosophy is to live in truth – to live in understanding.

▶ Herbs and spices play an important part in treating common ailments.

# THE ORIGINS OF AYURVEDA

The origins of Ayurveda are uncertain. It is recounted that thousands of years ago, men of wisdom or *rishis* (meaning seers) as they are known in India, were saddened by the suffering of humanity. They knew that ill health and short lives allowed man little time to consider his spirituality and to commune with the divine – with God. In the Himalayan mountains they prayed and meditated together, calling upon God to help them to relieve the plight of man, and God felt moved by compassion to give them the teachings that would enlighten them in the ways of healing illness and alleviating suffering upon the earth.

It is believed that these teachings are the Vedas, although this cannot be proven, due to the lack of historical records. A book called the *Atharva Veda* was one of the first detailed accounts of the system. From this, and perhaps other ancient writings, came the beginnings of Ayurvedic medicine, which has developed, changed and absorbed many

▲ Meditation has the power to calm the mind and opens the spirit to a greater consciousness. Indian *sadhus*, like the one pictured here, live a simple nomadic life, renouncing worldly goods to devote themselves to prayer and meditation.

other influences over hundreds of years to become what it is today. Due to the invasions of India, and the subsequent suppression of the original Indian way of life, several ancient texts have been lost or destroyed, but enough have

survived to ensure the continuation of the teachings.

Ayurveda is acknowledged as the traditional healing system of India. It comes from two Sanskrit words: *ayur*, meaning "life" and *veda*, meaning "knowing", and can be interpreted as "science of life". It is the oldest recorded healing system to remain intact and is extremely comprehensive. It has many different branches and has influenced traditional healing systems around the world.

The fundamental principles of Ayurveda are based upon the Indian philosophy called *Samkhya*, meaning "to know the Truth". The principle of Samkhya is that the basis of life is consciousness and that with the awakening of consciousness comes understanding about the way in which the universe works – including health and healing. Samkhya advocates that to live in the light of truth brings great illumination to the heart of man, and Ayurvedic practices are focused upon leading us toward that truth.

# THE INFLUENCE OF AYURVEDA

For centuries after the end of the Vedic era, Ayurvedic medicine developed into a comprehensive healing system. Its philosophy and techniques spread from India to China, Arabia, Persia and Greece, influencing Middle Eastern, Greek and Chinese healing practices. It is known that Ayurvedic practitioners reached ancient Athens, and it can be noted that the traditional Greek medicine based upon the bodily humours (characteristics), which will be discussed later in the book, is significantly similar to Ayurveda. Greek medicine strongly influenced the subsequent

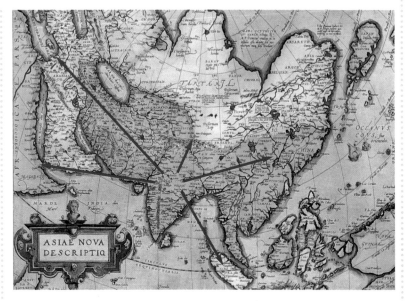

▲ Ayurveda travelled out of India and influenced many other countries with its ageless wisdom about living in the light of truth.

◀ Acupuncture is sometimes used in treatments, and it is likely that the technique originated in India and later spread to China.

development of traditional Western medicine, but it is difficult to say exactly to what degree the medical philosophy of Ayurveda was influential, or how much Ayurveda influenced Greek and European medicine.

The five elements in Chinese medicine appear to have come from Ayurveda. It is documented that the Indian medical system was brought to China by Indian Buddhist missionaries, many of whom were highly competent

Ayurvedic practitioners. The missionaries also travelled to South-East Asia and Tibet, influencing the people of these lands. Tibetan medicine, for example, is a combination of Ayurvedic practices and philosophy with a Tibetan Buddhist and shamanic influence.

# WHAT IS AYURVEDIC MEDICINE?

The main aim of Ayurvedic medicine (which is only one branch of Ayurveda) is to improve health and longevity, leaving the individual free to contemplate matters of the spirit and to follow a spiritual path. This does not mean that you have to be spiritual or religious to benefit from Ayurvedic medicine; the system is very practical in its applications and deals with all kinds of health problems, without spirituality ever being mentioned. Its main

▶ Ayurveda is primarily vegetarian. If meat must be eaten, choose a wild product rather than a commercially reared one, to ensure that the meat is as natural and organic as possible.

focus is nutrition, supported primarily by the use of herbs, massage and aromatic oils, but there are many complementary branches as well.

Ayurvedic philosophy encourages those who practise it to eat the fruits and seeds of the earth, rather than take the life of animals. Some animal products have been included in this introductory guide, but these should be used in moderation.

The branches of Ayurvedic medicine include specific diets, surgery, *jyotish* (Vedic astrology),

◀ Some of the biblical stories, such as that in which Mary Magdalene anoints the feet of Christ with oils, are Ayurvedic in nature. It is likely that this practice stemmed from the Ayurvedic tradition.

psychiatry and *pancha karma* (cleansing and detoxifying techniques). Yoga is not a branch of Ayurveda, but it shares the same roots and so the two are often practised together. Yoga includes meditation, mantras (prayer chants), yantras (contemplation of geometric visual patterns) and hatha yoga (practices for spirit, mind and body harmony). It is yoga that concentrates most precisely upon the more spiritual aspects of the Ayurvedic teachings.

# THE BRANCHES OF AYURVEDA

Wherever you go in the world, you will find people working with the elements, with the humours, the seasons and the planets. A humoral type is a mixture of physical, mental or emotional tendencies (influenced by karma in astrology). The physical and mental are not separated but are seen as two sides of the same coin.

In Ayurveda there are hot and cold people, thin and fat people, dry and moist people; these body types will have different tendencies emotionally, mentally and physically, and therefore will be affected by different types of food, herbs and oils.

The very important branch of Ayurvedic medicine called *pancha karma* focuses upon detoxification and uses steam baths, oelation (oiling), enemas and emesis (therapeutic vomiting), plus fasting. This may sound unsavoury to the Western mind, but pancha karma is a very effective way of cleansing the

◀ Certain gems correlate to planets – ruby to the sun and moonstone (left) to the moon for example.

system of toxins, especially those that are stubborn in their release, or have been held in the body for a long time. Pancha karma must only be performed by a qualified practitioner; at the moment it is seriously practised in India, Sri Lanka and the United States, but not yet in the United Kingdom.

Many things influence life on earth. The *jyotish* (Ayurvedic astrologer) assesses the birth chart and the current movement of the planets in the solar system to determine what may affect an

▶ It can be difficult to set aside the complexities of the material world and spend time in contemplation. Most people benefit from meditation or yoga, which can help to illuminate the pathway to inner peace.

individual's constitution. In order to alleviate potential aggravations from planetary influences, he or she may prescribe gems to wear on certain parts of the body. By following the advice of a jyotish, weak and strong areas of the birth chart can be worked on, to enhance the strengths, and strengthen the weaknesses.

# THE DOSHAS AND THE SEASONS

There are three doshas (basic types of people, in terms of constitution) – vata, pitta and kapha. They are influenced by the rhythms of nature, seasonal change and the time of year. Autumn is a time of change when leaves turn brown and dry out; vata is highest in autumn and early winter, and at times of dry, cold and windy weather. Pitta is highest in late spring, throughout the summer and during times of heat and humidity. Kapha is highest in the winter months and

◄ In spring, consider a cleansing fast to clear the body of any excess kapha that may have accumulated during the winter months. When kapha meets pitta in the spring, it can provide the conditions for colds and flu – the body's way of cleansing *ama* (toxins) and kapha from the system.

▼ Summer, the season of heat and activity, should be tempered with calming colours, soothing scents, and leisurely activities that enhance rest and relaxation.

WARMING UP/SPRING
pitta accumulating, kapha aggravated, vata neutral

HOT/SUMMER
vata accumulating, pitta aggravated, kapha decreasing

COOLING/AUTUMN
vata aggravated, pitta decreasing, kapha neutral

COLD/WINTER
vata decreasing, pitta neutral, kapha accumulating

questionnaire. If you discover that you are a dual doshic type, which is quite common, it is generally recommended that you vary your diet and lifestyle to suit the seasonal changes as described in the dual doshas section.

▼ In winter, kapha is accumulating, vata is decreasing and pitta is neutral. Winter is a time when people in colder climates tend to eat kapha-inducing foods that are more fatty and substantial. If you are a kapha dosha or have a kapha condition, include plenty of hot spices and warming drinks in your diet.

▲ Autumn is a time when the weather is changeable, which will increase levels of vata. Ensure that you have some stress-free time in comforting surroundings to help to keep vata in balance, especially if you are a vata dosha or have a vata condition.

during early spring, when the weather is cold and damp.

In Ayurvedic theory, the progress of a disease goes through several stages and this is reflected in seasonal influences upon the doshas. There is the process of accumulation of a dosha (when it is increasing), followed by a time

of aggravation (when it is at its highest point and can cause problems). There is a time of decrease (when it is lessening) and a neutral time, when it is passive (neither decreasing nor increasing). These four phases are associated with the seasons, bearing in mind that in different areas climatic conditions or seasonal variations may modify the general principles.

Use the questionnaire later in this book to discover your dosha – vata, pitta or kapha. Single doshic types can simply refer to whichever dosha scores the highest points on their

# FINDING YOUR BODY TYPE

This section outlines how you can identify your dosha or body type. Dosha means "that which tends to go out of balance easily". Your dosha is your bio-type or *prakruti* ("nature"). You are made up of a mixture of the five elements of ether, wind, fire, water and earth, and will display certain characteristics, depending upon your basic nature.

As well as your prakruti, you may also have a *vikruti*, which is your current state of mental or physical health. This develops throughout your life and may actually differ from your prakruti. It is important that you treat your vikruti first (how you are now), then go back to living with your prakruti. For example, you may have developed arthritis or back trouble over a long period of time, or you may be suffering from a cold or skin rash which lasts for a few days. Once you have cleared your condition, you can maintain your prakruti by preventative treatment which includes diet, massage, oils, colours and scents as well as an awareness of seasons and planets.

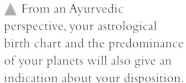 From an Ayurvedic perspective, your astrological birth chart and the predominance of your planets will also give an indication about your disposition.

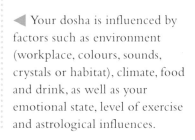 Your dosha is influenced by factors such as environment (workplace, colours, sounds, crystals or habitat), climate, food and drink, as well as your emotional state, level of exercise and astrological influences.

▲ The difference between your prakruti and vikruti can be compared with that between your astrological birth chart and the transits and progressions of the planets. These occur throughout your life and will exert strong influences upon you at certain times, modifying your fixed astrological birth chart as the planets move around the cosmos.

Apart from the three single doshas, there are four combinations, making a total of seven differing constitutional types: vata, pitta, kapha, vata/pitta (or pitta/vata), pitta/kapha (or kapha/pitta), kapha/vata (or vata/kapha), and vata/pitta/ kapha. These may be either out of balance or in a state of balance.

To discover your prakruti and vikruti, answer the questionnaire twice. Also ask other people who know you well to fill out the questionnaire for you, to give you as clear a picture of yourself as possible. The first time you fill out the questionnaire, you should concentrate upon your current condition – your vikruti – recording answers based upon the present and your recent health history.

You can discover your prakruti by answering the questionnaire a second time, this time with answers based upon your entire lifetime. Fill out the questionnaire with your complete history in mind. This will give you a better idea about the difference between your vikruti and your prakruti. Once the answers to the questionnaire have revealed both your vikruti and your prakruti (they may be the same, which is fine), the information in this book can be used to treat both. Follow whichever dosha scores most

highly (vata, pitta or kapha), whether you are trying to balance any excess or, having balanced your excess, are trying to maintain a state of balance. You can fill out the questionnaire again at regular intervals to monitor how you are progressing in balancing yourself. If, like many people, you are a dual type, refer to the section on dual doshas for advice on which plan is most suitable for you.

◄ Yoga can be a very helpful way of balancing the body and mind. Many of the yogic postures are named after things from the natural world, such as animals and trees. This is to help us to connect with these energies and so strengthen our connection to the dance of life in our universe. Yoga can be used as part of an exercise plan, to help to balance the doshas very effectively.

# ELEMENTAL ENERGIES

The elements are very important in Ayurveda. They descend from space (ether), down to air. Air descends into the fire element. Fire falls into the water element and water to earth, so that we move from the most rarefied of the elements (ether) to the most dense (earth). With this in mind, you will notice that the chart below follows a descending pattern of ether and air (vata), fire and water (pitta) and water and earth (kapha). Vata is a mixture of ether and air and is often

translated as "wind". In the creation story of Ayurveda, vata leads the other doshas, because its air-and-ether combination is the most rarefied. The elements move from the most refined down to the most dense. So, if vata is out of balance, this will generally make the others go out of balance as well.

Your age and the season of the year will also have an influence upon your doshic type. From childhood up to the teenage years you are

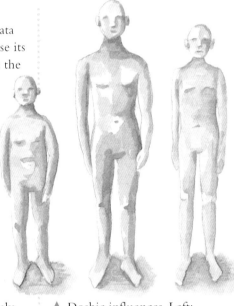

◀ People in the West are likely to have a problem with an excess of vata, even though there may be very little vata in the basic constitution. Vata relates to stress and the nervous system, and also to depletion, so will probably need treating to some extent.

▲ Doshic influences. Left: childhood, susceptibility to kapha conditions, such as colds. Centre: mid-life, risk of pitta conditions, such as digestive problems and headaches. Right: old age, susceptibility to vata conditions, such as arthritis and flatulence.

| ELEMENT | DOSHA | COSMIC LINK | PRINCIPLE | INFLUENCE |
|---|---|---|---|---|
| ether/air | vata | wind | change | activity/movement |
| fire/water | pitta | sun | conversion | metabolism/transformation |
| water/earth | kapha | moon | inertia | cohesion |

responses within the body. Everyone has all three doshas to some extent; it is their ratio to each other which is important, and it is this ratio which makes up our individuality. Each dosha plays an important role. For example movement (vata) without the stability of kapha would be chaos, and the inactivity of kapha without activity and movement would result in stagnation. Ayurveda sometimes refers to deficiencies, but usually considers the doshas in excess (too much pitta, for example). An excess of kapha would therefore indicate a need

▲ A vata type will be susceptible to excess "wind" or air, and will be potentially changeable, with a fairly active personality.

influenced by kapha; from your teens to the age of 50 or 60 you tend to come under the pitta influence, and from 50 to 60 onwards you enter the vata phase of life.

Each dosha has a particular energetic activity or principle, which influences certain

▼ A pitta type will have the potential for excess fire, like a hot sun, and will be able to transform or change things quite easily.

▲ A kapha type (water and earth) will be intuitive, sensitive and will dislike change but will be good at holding things together.

for a kapha-reducing eating and living plan, and the information in this introductory guide has been geared to deal with excesses in each of the doshas.

You will have an excess if you score significantly higher in one dosha than you do in the other two doshas.

# USING THE QUESTIONNAIRE

The questionnaire overleaf is designed to help you to assess your basic ratio of humoral factors. From this you can determine which diet, colours, exercise routines, crystals, oils and scents are most likely to suit you. By referring to the sections on which you score the most points, you will identify whether you are a vata, pitta or kapha dosha, or a combination type. Read the questions and, to discover your prakruti, tick those descriptions which apply to you in general terms. Allocate two ticks to the statement that is most applicable to you; use one tick for a description that could also apply, and if a description does not apply to you, leave it unticked.

As has already been explained, your current condition, or vikruti, may not be the same as your underlying constitution, or prakruti. If you wish to discover whether or not this is the case, go through the questions a second time, this time using crosses instead of ticks. To reveal your vikruti, answer the questions

according to how you have been feeling more recently, and how the descriptions relate to your current health or condition, including any illnesses or other changes you are experiencing.

When you are answering the questions, make sure that you focus either on your prakruti (general state throughout your life – ticks), or on your vikruti

▲ Vatas need to learn how to be still and grounded, because they tend to suffer from energy depletion, having the least amount of stamina.

(current or recent state – crosses). To avoid confusion, finish with one set of answers before you start to fill out and assess the questionnaire a second time.

If you wish, you can answer the questionnaire a third time, separating questions about the mind from questions about the body. Use circles and squares to record your answers. This will give you an idea as to whether your mind and your body are the same dosha or different. If they are different, you can follow the dietary advice for the body and the lifestyle advice for the mind, outlined in the relevant sections on doshas. For example, if you have a kapha body and a pitta mind, you would follow the kapha eating and exercise plan, including the massage technique, and ensure that you have cooling, soothing colours and a calm working and living environment with a certain amount of challenge to keep the pitta mind as balanced as possible.

Following the questionnaire are three sections headed "Vata",

◄ Gems are used in Ayurveda only with a prescription from a jyotish (Vedic or Hindu astrologer) or from an Ayurvedic physician. Set into a ring, they are worn on a specific finger.

▲ A jyotish will consult the planets and your astrological chart before working with crystals. Minerals should be treated with caution in case they are contra-indicated by your birth chart.

▶ Choose herbs carefully, ensuring that they are suitable for your particular doshic condition.

"Pitta" and "Kapha". Having discovered your vikruti (condition) or prakruti (constitution), turn to the pages relevant to your predominant dosha, for detailed advice on reducing any excess (vikruti), or for maintaining your true character (prakruti). When referring to the various sections, please read the information very carefully before you begin to put it into practice.

When using Ayurvedic medicinal herbs, remember to take them only as long as you are experiencing symptoms. Check that the herbs are still suited to your doshic needs on a regular basis.

When you begin to use any of the Ayurvedic prescriptions and techniques, do not be tempted to elaborate on them. Ayurveda is extremely complex and precise. For example, there are guidelines about the specific crystals that may be used to make a crystal infusion for each dosha. It is advisable that you do not make other infusions unless you are qualified or

◀ Choose oils according to your doshic condition.

experienced; crystals and gems can have a very powerful effect, so they must be used with respect and caution. If you find you do not feel good when wearing a particular crystal or gem, then you should remove it.

DISCOVER YOUR DOSHA
Mark the questionnaire with either a √ (= your general constitution – prakruti) or x (= your current or recent state – vikruti).

| | VATA | PITTA | KAPHA |
|---|---|---|---|
| HEIGHT | Very short, or tall and thin | Medium | Tall or short and sturdy |
| MUSCULATURE | Thin, prominent tendons | Medium/firm | Plentiful/solid |
| BODILY FRAME | Light, narrow | Medium frame | Large/broad |
| WEIGHT | Light, hard to gain | Medium weight | Heavy, gains easily |
| SWEAT | Minimal | Profuse, especially when hot | Moderate |
| SKIN | Dry, cold | Soft, warm | Moist, cool, possibly oily |
| COMPLEXION | Darkish | Fair, pink, red, freckles | Pale, white |
| HAIR AMOUNT | Average amount | Early thinning and greying | Plentiful |
| TYPE OF HAIR | Dry, thin, dark, coarse | Fine, soft, red, fair | Thick, lustrous, brown |
| SIZE OF EYES | Small, narrow or sunken | Average | Large, prominent |
| TYPE OF EYES | Dark brown or grey, dull | Blue/grey/hazel, intense | Blue, brown, attractive |
| TEETH AND GUMS | Protruding, receding gums | Yellowish, gums bleed | White teeth, strong gums |
| SIZE OF TEETH | Small or large, irregular | Average | Large |
| PHYSICAL ACTIVITY | Moves quickly, active | Moderate pace, average | Slow pace, steady |
| ENDURANCE | Low | Good | Very good |
| STRENGTH | Poor | Good | Very good |
| TEMPERATURE | Dislikes cold, likes warmth | Likes coolness | Aversion to cool and damp |
| STOOLS | Tendency to constipation | Tendency to loose stools | Plentiful, slow elimination |
| LIFESTYLE | Variable, erratic | Busy, tends to achieve a lot | Steady, can skip meals |
| SLEEP | Light, interrupted, fitful | Sound, short | Deep, likes plenty |
| EMOTIONAL TENDENCY | Fearful, anxious, insecure | Fiery, angry, judgmental | Greedy, possessive |
| MENTAL ACTIVITY | Restless, lots of ideas | Sharp, precise, logical | Calm, steady, stable |
| MEMORY | Good recent memory | Sharp, generally good | Good long term |
| REACTION TO STRESS | Excites very easily | Quick temper | Not easily irritated |
| WORK | Creative | Intellectual | Caring |
| MOODS | Change quickly | Change slowly | Generally steady |
| SPEECH | Fast | Clear, sharp, precise | Deep, slow |
| RESTING PULSE | | | |
|    WOMEN | Above 80 | 70–80 | Below 70 |
|    MEN | Above 70 | 60–70 | Below 60 |
| **Totals:** *Please add up* | **Vata** | **Pitta** | **Kapha** |

# AYURVEDIC TREATMENTS

The basis of Ayurvedic treatment is dietary. There are several very good Ayurvedic cookbooks on the market, and if you wish to learn more about Ayurvedic nutrition, it would be advisable to buy an appropriate recipe book.

The following pages are divided into sections outlining the basic characteristics of each type: their related emotions, the treatment systems associated with each dosha, and the symptoms of excess, together with information

about what to eat, which colours to wear, the scents and oils to use, the beneficial herbs and spices, and a tonic recipe for each type. Each section also includes a massage, some exercise tips, and an appropriate gem and crystal with which to work in order to help you to reduce any excess in your dosha(s) and also to maintain a balance. The principles are actually very simple, once you have become familiar with them. Follow the relevant plan, whether you are trying to reduce an excess or wish to maintain a balance in your system.

You can make up your own tonic recipes for your body type by combining ingredients from the appropriate eating plan, using recommended herbs and spices to enhance the healing.

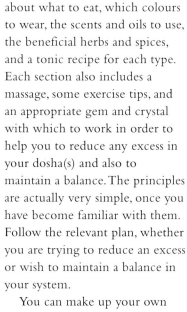

◄ In Ayurveda, the paths of cooking and treatment are intertwined, as certain foods, herbs and spices are used as tonics as well as for prevention and cure. They have a medicinal effect as well as a culinary use.

**THE DOSHAS AT WORK**
The differences and interdependencies between the various doshic types can be seen very clearly in a working environment. Here, vata people may produce imaginative ideas, but won't necessarily put them into action. They need pitta people to develop, engineer and sell. But pitta types want to be always active on the leading edge and so need kapha people to run

◀ Vata types benefit from putting some of their energy into creative pursuits.

the business from day to day.

Vata people are artistic, inventive, imaginative and sensitive and would be good in these roles at work. Vata types need regularity, routine, calm and warmth, and should avoid stress, and being ungrounded (avoiding flying or lots of travel, for example).

Pitta people need a challenge and something to develop or engineer without hindrance. They make good salespeople and enjoy developmental occupations, which are well suited to their basic nature.

Kapha people need stimulation and changes of routine to avoid inertia. They make good

◀ Kapha types need to change their routines sometimes and have fun.

managers because they are steady and reliable. They will tend always to be there when you need them.

Each individual will have specific qualities to bring to the workplace, and business benefits from finding the right people for the right jobs. The key to a successful company is to employ all three doshic types to ensure a balanced team.

▲ Pitta types need to relax and slow down, taking time to appreciate themselves and others.

**DOSHIC QUALITIES**
Vata: creative, good ideas.
Pitta: activators, good promoters.
Kapha: reliable, good managers.

# VATA

THE VATA BODY TYPE IS USUALLY thin and narrow. Vatas do not gain weight easily and are often restless by nature, especially when they are busy and active. They have dry hair and cool skin and a tendency to feel the cold. Their levels of energy are erratic, and they have to be careful not to exhaust themselves due to lack of consistency. They may find it hard to relax, which can lead to an over-active mind and insomnia.

Vata symptoms will be changeable, cold in

their nature and therefore worse in cold weather. Any pain will worsen during change. Vata

◀ Vata people should eat warming food which is earthy and sweet, with the emphasis upon cooked foods, such as this bowl of dhal, rather than salads.

people can suffer from wind, low back pain, arthritis and nerve disorders. When there is excess vata in the system, fear, depression and nervousness will develop. Whenever there are repressed emotions, vata will also be aggravated which, in turn, will affect the flora and fauna present in the digestive system, causing not only a degree of discomfort and bloating, but also a lessening of the effectiveness of the immune system.

Vata types, because of their restless nature, require a regular intake of nourishment and should sit down to eat or drink at regular times. Exercise should be in moderation, maintaining a gentle routine that will help to focus the mind and body to work in unison. Routine and regularity help to ground excess vata.

ELEMENTS: ether and air.
CLIMATE: dry and cold.
PRINCIPLE: movement.
EMOTIONS: fearful, anxious, sensitive, nervous, changeable.
SYSTEMS MOST AFFECTED BY EXCESS VATA: the nervous system and the colon.
SYMPTOMS OF EXCESS VATA: flatulence, back pain, circulation problems, dry skin, fearfulness, arthritis, constipation and nerve disorders.

▶ In summer vata is accumulating as the heat of the sun begins to dry everything out. Keep your skin moist with natural creams in order to prevent your skin drying out too.

# DIETARY RECOMMENDATIONS

Vata people should avoid all fried foods and should eat at regular intervals. To reduce excess vata, follow the vata diet and recommendations in your eating and living plan and avoid foods and other items not listed as much as possible. If including animal products, these should be used in moderation.

### HERBS AND SPICES
Almond essence, asafoetida (hing), basil leaves, bay leaves,

▼ *Ginger, cardamom pods, coriander, vanilla pods, oregano, cloves, black mustard seeds and asafoetida (hing).*

▲ *Wheat grains, pumpkin seeds and long grain rice.*

black mustard seeds, cardamom pods, cloves, coriander (cilantro), cumin, dill, fennel, fresh ginger, marjoram, mint, nutmeg, oregano, paprika, parsley, peppermint, spearmint, tarragon, thyme, turmeric and vanilla – of these, asafoetida is especially good for vatas. It helps with the digestion of food and reduces wind, which is particularly useful if you eat pulses and beans.

### GRAINS AND SEEDS
Oats (cooked), pumpkin seeds, quinoa, rice (all varieties), sesame seeds, sprouted wheat bread, sunflower seeds and wheat.

### NUTS
Almonds, brazil nuts, cashews, hazelnuts, macadamias, pecans, pine nuts, pistachios and walnuts.

### MEAT AND FISH
Beef, chicken, duck, eggs, seafish, shrimps and turkey. Vatas may benefit from eating meat and fish because these foods are grounding and strengthening.

### VEGETABLES
Artichokes, asparagus, beetroot, carrots, courgettes (zucchini), cucumber, daikon radish, green

▼ *Cashews, pine nuts, pecans, almonds and pistachios.*

▲ *Eggs and mackerel.*

beans, leeks, okra, olives, onions (cooked), parsnips, pumpkins, radishes, spinach (cooked), swede (rutabagas), sweet potatoes, tomatoes (cooked) and watercress.

▼ *Cows' milk, cottage cheese and goats' cheese.*

## FRUIT

Apricots, avocados, bananas, berries, cherries, coconuts, dates, fresh figs, grapefruit, grapes, lemons, limes, mangoes, melons, oranges, peaches, pineapples, plums, rhubarb and strawberries.

## DAIRY PRODUCTS

Cows' milk, cottage cheese, goats' milk, goats' cheese and soft cheese – all to be taken in moderation.

## COOKING OILS

Unrefined sesame oil.

## DRINKS

Apricot juice, berry juice, carrot juice, cider, ginger tea, grape juice, grapefruit juice, hot dairy

▼ *Unrefined sesame oil.*

▲ *Carrots, daikon radish, olives, courgettes (zucchini), asparagus, artichokes and watercress.*

drinks, lemon balm tea, lemonade, orange juice, peach juice, peppermint tea, pineapple juice, rosehip tea and spearmint tea.

▼ *Orange juice.*

# AROMAS AND MASSAGE OILS

Vata people tend to benefit more than either of the other doshas from massage, and they should consider massaging their feet, hands and head every morning and having a regular massage once a week. Vata aromas are warm and sweet, and the most appropriate massage oil for the vata personality is warmed sesame oil. In general, all oil is good for vata and vata types, and if vata is seriously out of balance, the once-weekly massage may be increased to three times a week.

Essential oils must be diluted. Do not put them directly on your

skin or take them internally. It is advisable not to use the same essential oil for more than two weeks; interchange your essential oils so that you do not create a toxic build-up or overload of one fragrance. If you are pregnant or have a diagnosed medical

 Mix 7–10 drops of your chosen essential oil with 25ml/ 1fl oz/⅛ cup carrier oil, and pour oil on to your hands first, to warm it before you begin.

condition, do not use any essential oil without consulting a qualified practitioner.

Warm, calming or earthy essential oils are the most suitable for vata. These include camphor (which can be an irritant, so test yourself for sensitivity first), eucalyptus, ginger, sandalwood and jatamansi (a spikenard species from India).

## VATA MASSAGE

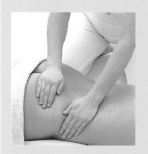

**1** A vata massage should be gentle.

**2** Keep the actions soothing and relaxing.

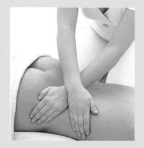

**3** Use stroking movements.

**4** Oil and ease areas of dry, tight skin.

# COLOURS

Vata individuals benefit from most of the pastel colours and from earthy colours that are gentle and warm to look at, such as ochres, browns and yellows.

### OCHRE
A warm, friendly but relaxing colour, ochre draws the energy down through the system, helping the vata individual to feel more solid and steady.

### BROWN
A solid, reliable colour that helps to ground the vata type, stabilizing any tendency to flightiness, holding the emotions in place, and helping the vata personality to consolidate and concentrate.

### YELLOW
A warming, enlivening colour, yellow is linked to the mind and the intellect. It

▶ Warm yellows are suitable for vata people.

helps to keep the vata mentality alert by focusing the mind and calming any rising emotions.

### MAKING A COLOUR INFUSION
Take a piece of thin cotton or silk. The fabric should be warm yellow in colour and sufficiently thin to allow the light to penetrate. Wrap it around a small transparent (not coloured) jar or bottle filled with

▲ Make a colour infusion to treat symptoms of excess vata – entering a potentially stressful situation, for example. Choose clothes and accessories that will be warming and comforting.

spring water. Leave it outside in the sunlight for about four hours. Remove the fabric and drink the infusion to encourage a sense of warmth and well-being. Vata infusions should not be stored in the fridge, but kept at room temperature.

# GEMS AND CRYSTALS

Gems and crystals have healing qualities that can be utilized in Ayurvedic medicine. Their powers are taken seriously by the jyotish (Vedic astrologer), who can determine which gems or crystals to use depending on the circumstances of your life chart.

Topaz is a warm stone that traditionally dispels fear, making it an ideal stone for vata as it calms emotionalism and anxiety. Wear topaz whenever you want to feel confident and in control. Amethyst is an appropriate crystal to wear when you want to balance vata. It promotes clarity of mind and thought, and will help you to radiate a sense of harmony.

There may be times when it is advisable to remove all crystals – when you find circumstances in your life are changing for the worse. This indicates that your birth chart or constitution does not require the healing qualities of a particular crystal, or that it is highlighting some area of your birth chart in a negative way.

### MAKING A CRYSTAL INFUSION

Before making a crystal infusion, it is advisable to cleanse your crystal first. (Crystals that are used for infusions should ideally be cleansed before and after each use.) To make a crystal infusion, take the cleansed crystal and hold it in your hands, imagining that the crystal is full of peace and calm. Place the crystal in a clear glass bowl, cover it with spring water, and leave it in the sunlight for about four hours. Remove the

TOURMALINE QUARTZ

SMOKY QUARTZ

CLEAR QUARTZ

AVENTURINE

MILKY QUARTZ

CITRINE

RUTILATED QUARTZ

ROSE QUARTZ

AMETHYST

◀ Amethyst, from the quartz family, is good for vata. This, and other crystals from this family, are the safest for infusions.

crystal and bottle the spring water. Drink the infusion prior to any mentally demanding tasks. It will aid clarity of mind and help to reduce any stress that might arise as a result of pressure. You can keep the infusion for 24 hours, after which it should be discarded. Store your infusion away from domestic appliances and electrical equipment.

▶ Amethyst is an ideal healing stone, as it balances and quietens the mind. You may become aware of an increased imagination and a greater ability to visualize clearly.

## CLEANSING A CRYSTAL

**1** To cleanse your amethyst, dissolve a teaspoon of sea salt in a clear glass bowl filled with spring water.

**2** Place the crystal in the water and leave it to stand for about eight hours (or you can leave it overnight).

**3** Rinse it in spring water, visualizing any residues that were being held in the crystal being washed away.

# EXERCISE AND TONIC

Vata is cold in nature and so benefits from warmth and comfort. Make your own warming tonic drinks for cold windy days by combining ingredients from the vata eating plan. Be aware that sugar weakens the immune system and vatas, with their tendency to stress (another immune suppressor), need to be particularly wary of

▶ Meditation in half or full lotus keeps the spine straight and energy flowing freely.

sugary and refined foods, choosing naturally sweet-tasting foods, such as fruit, instead.

Vata people benefit from gentle, relaxing forms of exercise. They are the most easily exhausted of the various categories, so they should be careful not to overdo things. Examples of gentle exercise include walking, yoga and slow swimming. In essence, it is not so much the form of exercise that you take, but rather the way in which you take it. With vata,

▲ Relaxing forms of yoga, swimming and calming exercise are ideal for the vata individual.

the exercise routine should be gentle; with this in mind, vata types can undertake most sports and activities.

Yoga stretches will gently lengthen your muscles and increase your flexibility. If you do not practise yoga as a form of exercise, you may find that achieving a half or full lotus for meditation is too difficult. If this is the case, you can use a specifically designed meditation stool, or place some firm cushions underneath you. Push your bent knees on to the floor, then tuck your feet in towards you on the floor, forming a solid triangular base with your legs.

## FRESH GINGER AND LEMON TEA

This fresh ginger and lemon tea is a delicious tonic for a vata.

*1 lemon*
*A small piece of fresh ginger (about the size of a thumbnail)*
*Spring water*
*Raw honey or fructose (fruit sugar)*

**1** Wash the lemon and then cut it into thin slices, leaving the peel on.

**2** Peel the piece of fresh ginger and slice it finely.

**3** Place the lemon and ginger slices in a small teapot.

**4** Add boiling spring water. Stir. Sweeten with honey or fructose.

# PITTA

THE PITTA BODY TYPE IS USUALLY OF average build and nicely proportioned. Pittas like their food and have a healthy appetite. The hair is usually straight, fine and fair (but dark-haired people can also be pitta types). People with red hair will automatically have some level of pitta within their nature. Like the fire element, their temperament can be intense, and when it manifests in excess this can lead to intolerance and irritability.

Pitta skin will have a tendency to be sensitive to the sun, and pitta types will need to be careful how much time they spend in direct sunlight. The fiery nature of the sun will sometimes inflame the pitta person, leading to skin rashes, freckles and sunburn. All hot and humid weather will aggravate pitta. Cool showers, cool environments and cooling drinks (but not ice-cold ones) will help to alleviate any steaming temperatures and calm pitta down.

People of this nature can be impatient, because their highly active and alert minds can make them aggressive in situations that are irritating to them. However, pitta people can also have a very good sense of humour and a warm personality. They make good promoters and salespeople because they like challenge. It is good for pitta to have the opportunity to rise to a challenge, but they must ensure that after frantic activity some time is dedicated to rest and recuperation, something that pitta types will tend to avoid.

Pitta people should choose foods that are soothing and avoid hot, spicy dishes.

ELEMENTS: fire and water.
CLIMATE: hot and moist.
PRINCIPLE: transformation.
EMOTIONS: hate, anger, intolerance, impatience, jealousy, humour, intelligence, warm-heartedness.
SYSTEMS AFFECTED BY EXCESS PITTA: skin, metabolism, small intestines, eyes, liver, hair of the head.
SYMPTOMS OF EXCESS PITTA: skin disorders, acidity, sun-sensitivity, premature hair loss or loss of hair colour, diarrhoea.

▶ Pitta types benefit from spending time in shaded and naturally calming surroundings.

# DIETARY RECOMMENDATIONS

The pitta person should avoid all hot, spicy and sour foods, as they will aggravate this dosha; they should also avoid all fried foods. Any heating of food and drink will increase pitta within the system, so pitta types should eat more raw than cooked foods. As a primarily vegetarian system, Ayurveda does not advocate the eating of animal products, especially for the pitta dosha, so although some meats and other animal products have been included in the following list, they should really be used in strict moderation – if at all – by

▼ *Dill, dried coriander leaves and spearmint.*

▲ *Sunflower seeds, basmati rice, barley and rice cakes.*

the pitta personality.

To reduce excess pitta in the system (vikruti), or to maintain balance within your personality (prakruti) because you are a pitta type by nature, include the following foods in your eating and living plan, and avoid any items that are not listed as much as you can.

## HERBS AND SPICES
Aloe vera juice (not to be used in pregnancy), basil leaves, cinnamon, coriander (cilantro), cumin, dill, dulse, fennel, fresh ginger, hijiki, mint leaves and spearmint.

## GRAINS AND SEEDS
Barley, basmati rice, flax seeds, psyllium seeds, rice cakes, sunflower seeds, wheat, wheat bran and white rice.

## BEANS AND PULSES
Aduki beans, black beans, black-eyed beans, chick peas (garbanzos), kidney beans, lentils (red and brown), lima beans, mung beans, pinto beans, soya beans, split peas, tempeh and tofu.

## NUTS
Almonds (peeled) and coconuts.

▼ *Black-eyed beans, mung beans, soya beans, aduki beans and chick peas (garbanzos).*

▲ *Coconut and almonds.*

MEAT AND FISH
Chicken, freshwater fish, rabbit,
turkey and venison.

VEGETABLES
Artichokes, asparagus, broccoli,
Brussels sprouts, butternut squash,
cabbages, carrots, cauliflowers,
courgettes (zucchini), cucumber,
celery, fennel, green beans, green
peppers, Jerusalem artichokes,
kale, leafy greens, leeks, lettuces,
mushrooms, onions (cooked),
parsnips, peas, pumpkins, spinach
(cooked), swede (rutabagas), sweet
potatoes, white potatoes and
winter squash. Pittas should eat
salads regularly, and eat raw rather
than cooked vegetables.

FRUIT
Apples, apricots, avocadoes,
berries, cherries, dates, figs,

▲ *Melon, mango, avocado,
blackberries, apricot, cherries
and pineapple.*

mangoes, melons, oranges,
pears, pineapples, plums,
pomegranates, prunes, quinces,
raisins, red grapes and water-
melons. Always make sure that the
fruits are fully ripe, very sweet
and fresh.

▼ *Walnut oil, sunflower oil, and
olive oil.*

▲ *Unsalted butter, yoghurt and
cottage cheese.*

DAIRY PRODUCTS
Cottage cheese, cows' milk, diluted
yoghurt, ghee, goats' milk, mild
soft cheese and unsalted butter
may be consumed in moderation.

COOKING OILS
Olive oil, sunflower oil, soya and
walnut oil. As with dairy
products, these oils should be
used in moderation.

DRINKS
Apple juice, apricot juice, cool
dairy drinks, grape juice, mango
juice, mixed vegetable juice, soya
milk, vegetable bouillon,
elderflower tea, hibiscus tea,
jasmine tea, marshmallow tea,
nettle tea, spearmint tea and
strawberry tea. Juices should be
cool but not ice-cold.

# AROMAS AND MASSAGE OILS

Essential oils for pitta include honeysuckle, jasmine, sandalwood and vetiver. They must be diluted and should never be taken internally. Avoid a toxic build-up by interchanging the oils every two weeks. If you are pregnant or have a diagnosed medical condition, consult a practitioner before using essential oils.

▶ Pitta individuals require a small amount of oil. Choose cooling carrier oils, such as coconut oil.

## PITTA MASSAGE

**1** Mix 7–10 drops of your chosen essential oil with 25ml/1 fl oz/⅛ cup carrier oil.

**2** Pitta massage should be calming and relaxing. Use deep and varied movements.

**3** Be gentle wherever there may be inflamed tissues, such as areas of stiffness or soreness.

**4** Use calm, slow, sweeping movements without any sudden changes in direction.

# COLOURS

If you are experiencing symptoms of excess pitta, such as irritability or impatience, or on occasions when you know that you are going to have a busy and active day ahead of you, balance your system by wearing natural fibres in cooling and calming colours, such as green, blue, violet or any quiet pastel shade.

## BLUE
Blue is a soothing, healing colour which is ideal for the active pitta type. Blue is linked to spiritual consciousness and helps the pitta type to remain open and calm without being over-stimulated.

## GREEN
Green, an integral colour of the natural world, brings harmonious feelings to the pitta personality, having the ability to soothe emotions and calm passionate feelings.

▶ Wear blues in silks and cottons.

## VIOLET
Violet is a refined colour that soothes and opens the mind, and increases awareness of spiritual issues.

### MAKING A COLOUR INFUSION
Take a piece of thin, translucent cotton or silk in violet or light blue. Wrap it

▲ A blue colour infusion will help to clear the system of pressure build-up.

around a small transparent (not coloured) bottle or jar filled with spring water. Leave it outside in dappled sunlight, not in direct sun, for six hours. Remove the fabric, and drink the infusion to encourage the sensation of peace and harmony.

# GEMS AND CRYSTALS

When you want to reduce excess pitta, wear pearls or a mother-of-pearl ring set in silver upon the ring finger of your right hand. Pearls have the ability to reduce inflammatory conditions, including heated emotions. Ideally, natural pearls should be worn, although cultured pearls are acceptable. The most harmonious day to put on your pearls is a Monday (the moon's day) during a new moon. Do not wear pearls when you have a kapha condition, such as a cold.

The moonstone has the ability to calm emotions and is soft and cooling, being feminine in orientation. It can help to pacify the pitta personality.

▲ Moonstone is a suitable crystal to use when you need to reduce excess pitta.

### MAKING A MOONSTONE INFUSION

**1** Take a stone specimen that has already been cleansed. Put it into a clear glass bowl and fill it with fresh spring water until the stone is covered.

**2** Leave the bowl outside to stand under the light of a full moon for three hours – or overnight if the night is calm and clear.

**3** Remove the moonstone (remember to cleanse it after use) and pour the liquid into a clear glass.

**4** Drink the moonstone infusion first thing in the morning, to assure yourself of a harmonious day.

# EXERCISE AND TONIC

Cooling drinks such as fruit and vegetable juices are ideal tonics for the pitta constitution.

Pittas require a moderate amount of exercise, which should involve some element of vigour and challenge – jogging, team sports and certain martial arts. It is not so much what you do but how you do it that is important here. Pitta exercise should not overstimulate the body; any exercise should be kept in line with an average amount of effort and challenge. You should avoid going to such extremes that your pitta nature gets carried away and you overdo it!

▼ Pittas should play games for enjoyment rather than to win.

### ORANGE AND ELDERFLOWER INFUSION

This orange and elderflower infusion is a light and delicate alternative to a cordial. Cordials are made by boiling the ingredients together, which is not appropriate for pitta types because of the heat required for the process.

1 large sweet orange
2 large fresh elderflower heads
Fresh spearmint
300ml / ½ pint spring water
Fructose (fruit sugar) to taste

**1** Wash the orange in spring water. Cut into slices and place in a tall jug.

**2** Add the elderflower heads and a sprig of spearmint.
**3** Pour in spring water, stir gently and leave it to stand for one hour.
**4** Stir again, strain and add fructose (fruit sugar) to taste.
**5** Top with sprigs of fresh spearmint, and sip slowly.

# KAPHA

THE KAPHA BODY TYPE IS WELL built, with a tendency to weight problems, especially if an exercise programme is not followed to keep the kapha active and moving. Kapha people are naturally athletic but need motivation. They are sensitive and emotional and require understanding, otherwise they tend to turn to food as an emotional support. They should ensure that what they eat is suitable for their body type.

Their hair will be thick, fine and wavy, their skin smooth, and their eyes large and attractive.

ELEMENTS: water and earth.
CLIMATE: cold and damp.
PRINCIPLE: cohesion.
EMOTIONS: stubbornness, greed, jealousy, possessiveness, lethargy, reliability and methodical behaviour, kindliness, motherliness.
SYSTEMS MOST AFFECTED BY EXCESS KAPHA: joints, lymphatics, body fluids and mucous membranes throughout the body.
SYMPTOMS OF EXCESS KAPHA: congestion, bronchial/nasal discharge, sluggish digestion, nausea, slow mental responses, idleness, desire for sleep, excess weight, fluid retention.

▲ Kapha food should be light, dry, hot and stimulating. Opt for cooked foods, such as this hot and spicy vegetable curry, in preference to salads.

Kapha people are inclined to be slow and steady, methodical and pragmatic, with a dislike of change. They make good managers, because they like to be reliable and available. They act like an anchor in a business, as they have an innate organizing ability.

Bright, strong and invigorating colours will help to reduce excess kapha and stimulate a system that may be sluggish and dull.

▶ Because kapha individuals have a tendency towards inertia, they need motivation, so early morning exercise outdoors is a good start to the day.

# DIETARY RECOMMENDATIONS

Kapha people should focus upon cooked food, but can have some salads occasionally. They should avoid fats and oils, unless these are hot and spicy. Dairy products, sweet, sour and salty tastes and an excessive intake of wheat will also aggravate kapha. Although some meats and animal products have been included, they should really be used in strict moderation.

To reduce excess kapha (vikruti), or to maintain balance because you are a kapha dosha (prakruti), include the following items in your eating plan and try to avoid foods not listed.

▼ *Buckwheat, couscous, barley and pumpkin seeds.*

▲ *Black-eyed beans, aduki beans and chick peas (garbanzos).*

## HERBS AND SPICES

Asafoetida (hing), black pepper or pippali (an Indian pepper), chilli pepper, coriander leaves (cilantro), dry ginger, garlic, horseradish, mint leaves, mustard, onions, parsley, radishes or any other hot spices. (Hot spices should be avoided if you suffer from gastro intestinal ulcers.)

## GRAINS AND SEEDS

Barley, buckwheat, corn, couscous, oat bran, polenta, popcorn (plain), rye, sprouted wheat bread, toasted pumpkin seeds and toasted sunflower seeds. As the fat content in nuts is high,

this is a food that should be avoided by kapha types. However, toasted seeds, eaten in small quantities, can be used instead of nuts. To toast seeds, place them on a baking tray and put under a hot grill for a few moments, until the seeds start to brown. Shake the tray out occasionally to ensure that the seeds are browned evenly. Toasted seeds are a delicious addition to couscous, and can be sprinkled as a topping over other cooked foods and salads.

## BEANS AND PULSES

Aduki beans, black-eyed beans, chick peas (garbanzos), lima

▼ *Eggs and shrimps.*

beans, pinto beans, red lentils, split peas and tempeh.

### MEAT AND FISH
Eggs, freshwater fish, turkey, rabbit, shrimps and venison.

### VEGETABLES
Most kapha vegetables should be cooked. Artichokes, asparagus, aubergines (eggplant), beetroot, broccoli, Brussels sprouts, cabbage, carrots, cauliflower, celery, daikon radish, fennel, green beans, Jerusalem artichokes, kale, leeks, lettuce, mushrooms, okra, onions, peas, peppers, radishes, spinach, swede (rutabagas), sweetcorn, turnips, watercress and white potatoes.

▼ *Apples, prunes, cranberries, apricots and pomegranates.*

▲ *Artichokes, mushrooms, onions, asparagus, green beans and runner beans.*

### FRUITS
Apples, apricots, berries, cherries, cranberries, peaches, pears, pomegranates, prunes and raisins.

▼ *Almond, sunflower and corn oil.*

### COOKING OILS
Corn, almond or sunflower oil may be used in small quantities.

### DRINKS
Fruit drinks should not contain sugar or additives. If you are buying juices from a retail outlet, ensure that the ingredients are fresh and contain no additives or sweeteners. Sweeteners include sugar substitutes, such as saccharin. Hot drinks that are recommended for kapha include black tea, carrot juice, cranberry juice, grape juice, mango juice, mixed vegetable juice, nettle tea, passionflower tea, raspberry tea and wine (a very small amount of dry red or white).

▼ *Carrot juice and cranberry juice.*

# AROMAS AND MASSAGE OILS

Kapha individuals require minimal oil or none at all with massage, using instead a natural, unscented talcum powder which can be purchased from most health food stores. If an essential oil is used at all, the ones that are good for kapha individuals include eucalyptus, cinnamon, orange peel (this can cause sun sensitivity, so avoid strong sunlight after a massage with orange peel), ginger and myrrh. All of these oils are stimulating

▲ If you are going to use essential oils, choose a stimulating one such as ginger, diluting it in a base of almond oil to avoid burning. However, a natural talcum powder is more suitable.

and it would be advisable, after diluting approximately 7–10 drops of essential oil in 25ml/1 fl oz/⅛ cup carrier oil, to test an area of skin first for sensitivity.

Essential oils must be diluted and should not be taken internally. It is advisable not to use the same essential oil for more than two weeks. If you are pregnant or have a diagnosed medical condition, do not use any essential oil without consulting a qualified practitioner.

## KAPHA MASSAGE

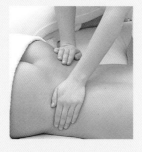

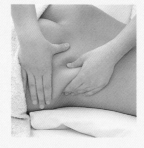

**1** Kapha massage needs to be fairly vigorous, to stimulate a sluggish metabolism and encourage regularity.

**2** Use fast and strong movements, using very little oil or none at all – use natural talcum powder instead.

**3** Massage that encourages lymphatic drainage is often beneficial, so focus on the hip and groin area.

**4** Another major lymph gland area is around the armpits. Massaging here releases any congestion.

# COLOURS

Kapha individuals benefit from the warm and stimulating colours of the spectrum.

Whenever you experience symptoms such as lethargy and sluggishness, which suggest excess kapha, or if you need to be particularly active, wear bright, invigorating colours. You will feel more inspired when you wear colours that tend to enliven the kapha personality.

### RED
Red is the colour of blood and will increase circulation as well as being energizing and positive. It should be used sparingly, to avoid over-stimulation of kapha, which would then lead to excess pitta.

### ORANGE
Orange is a warming, nourishing colour which feeds the sexual organs. Its glowing colour helps to remove congestion in the system.

▶ Pink accessories will boost energy.

### PINK
Warm, comforting pinks gently stimulate kapha into activity. Being a softer colour than red, pink may be worn without ill-effect for longer periods.

### MAKING A COLOUR INFUSION
Take a piece of thin cotton or silk. The fabric should be naturally dyed to a warm pink and sufficiently translucent to allow the light to penetrate.

▲ A pink colour infusion will help to bring love and warmth into your day.

Wrap it around a transparent (not coloured) small bottle containing spring water. Stand it in full sunlight or upon a windowsill with the window open so that the light can fall naturally upon the bottle, and leave it for about four hours. Remove the fabric and drink the contents of the bottle. You can store the infusion for up to 24 hours, after which it should be discarded.

# GEMS AND CRYSTALS

Lapis lazuli is a suitable crystal with which to reduce excess kapha. Known as the heavenly stone, it will help kapha individuals to raise their bodily vibrations, from their tendency to be dense and slow to a more refined and spiritual resonance.

## CRYSTAL INFUSION

Cleanse your lapis lazuli prior to making an infusion. Hold the lapis in your hands for a few moments, visualizing clarity and inspiration. The crystal is now ready for use. Place it in a clear glass bowl and cover with spring water. Leave it outside in the sunlight for about four hours. Remove the crystal and bottle the infused spring water. Drink small amounts throughout the day to ensure a continued rising of your spirits towards enlivened and motivated action.

▼ Ruby is a suitable gem to use in order to reduce excess kapha. Wear a ruby set in gold or silver, to encourage strength and resolve.

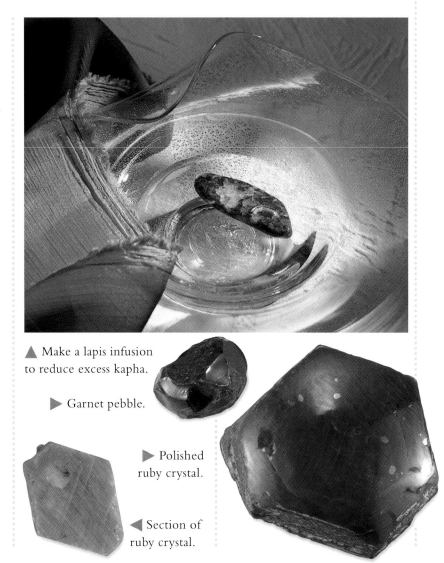

▲ Make a lapis infusion to reduce excess kapha.

▶ Garnet pebble.

▶ Polished ruby crystal.

◀ Section of ruby crystal.

48

# EXERCISE AND TONIC

Kapha types may well avoid this page because it suggests exercise! However, kapha people must address their natural aversion to physical activity – it will make all the difference to cleansing excess kapha and so make room for their inner beauty to shine through.

◀ Kapha people need to ensure that they have vigorous exercise, such as aerobics.

## SPICED YOGI TEA

Spiced yogi tea is a delicious, warming drink which will help to reduce excess kapha.

*½ teaspoon dry ginger*
*4 whole cardamom pods*
*5 cloves*
*1 large cinnamon stick*
*A pinch of black pepper or pippali (Indian long pepper)*
*600ml/1 pint/2½ cups spring water*
*30ml/2tbsp goats' milk or organic soya milk*

**1** Mix the spices together in a saucepan.
**2** Add the spring water and boil off half the liquid.
**3** Turn off the heat and add the goats' milk or soya milk.
**4** Stir and strain the liquid. Serve hot.

Kapha individuals will tend to shy away from vigorous exercise and so a certain amount of self-discipline is required. Once a regular exercise routine is established, however, the kapha type will enjoy and benefit from the enlivened and energetic feeling that activity and exercise brings. Examples of vigorous exercise suited to the kapha type include running, fast swimming, aerobics and fitness training. If unused to exercise, start with a gentle routine, and seek guidance from a qualified trainer.

It is advisable to increase the level of exercise in colder weather when extra stimulation is required, and this should take the form of a regular routine which really pushes the kapha type.

# DUAL DOSHAS

If, when you answer the questionnaire in the introduction, you find that you score twice as many points on any one type as on the other two, this means that you will be predominantly that type. For example, a score of 30 points on kapha and 5 or 10 on the others would indicate that you are a kapha type. If there is a closer gap – perhaps 30 points for kapha and 20 for pitta – you would be a kapha/pitta type.

If you are a dual type, read the following information.

▼ Vata/pitta – pitta/vata herbs include basil, coriander (cilantro), cumin seeds, fennel, mint, turmeric and vanilla pods.

VATA/PITTA – PITTA/VATA
Vata/pitta is a combination of ether/air and fire/water elements.

▼ Eat sweet, ripe fruits such as melons and oranges when in season if you are a vata/pitta type.

If you belong to this dual type, refer to both the vata and the pitta eating and living plans. Choose items from the pitta plan during the spring and summer months and during hot, humid weather. Follow the vata plan during the autumn and winter months and during cold, dry weather. For example, pungent foods aggravate pitta, but can help to calm vata (because vata is cold), which is why the plans need to be changed in accordance with weather, your health or other factors.

Eat your vegetables in season, and mostly cooked and flavoured with appropriate vata spices to minimize aggravation of vata and pitta. Only small amounts of bitter vegetables should be used. Among foods suitable for the vata/pitta type are broccoli, cauliflower, cucumber, endive, kale, onion (cooked), plantain, coconut, sweet oranges, apricots and other sweet fruits. Teas that are beneficial include elderflower, fennel, lemon balm and rosehip teas. Herbs and spices for vata/pitta – pitta/vata include fresh basil, caraway, cardamom, cumin, fennel, garam masala, spearmint and vanilla.

The nature of vata is change and so for this reason, when you become more familiar with

▶ Fennel is useful for digestive disorders.

the doshic influences that the climate has upon you as an individual, you may want to be more flexible with the doshic recommendations. Remember that it is not only climate that affects the doshas, but absolutely everything that touches your life. In working and personal relationships, try to adopt the approach recommended for your dosha. If you are a vata dosha, your moods may fluctuate, and

▲ Your lifestyle can be affected by your health. Pitta or vata doshas should find time to create a calming and restful ambience in which to relax and wind down.

you need to try to approach things with more consistency. If you are a pitta dosha you may get irritated and be abrupt, so do your best to be tolerant and patient. If you are a kapha dosha you may be stubborn, possessive and jealous. Try to be more trusting and flexible.

## PITTA/KAPHA – KAPHA/PITTA

This is a combination of fire, water and earth elements. If you are this dual type, follow the kapha eating and living plan during the winter months and during cold, damp weather and

▼ Pitta/kapha – kapha/pitta foods include curry leaves or powder, garam masala, mint, orange peel oil and rosewater.

follow the pitta plan during the summer months and hot humid weather.

Choose foods that are pungent and astringent, such as onions, celery, lemons, dandelion, mustard greens and watercress, and eat your fruit and vegetables fresh and in season. All fruit juices should be diluted in water or milk. Suitable teas for the pitta/kapha – kapha/pitta type include bancha twig, blackberry,

▲ Vegetables for the pitta/kapha diet include celery and onion.

dandelion, jasmine, licorice (not to be used if you suffer from high blood pressure or oedema) and spearmint. Herbs, spices and flavourings for the pitta/kapha type include coriander, dill leaves, fennel, kudzu, orange peel, parsley, rosewater and spearmint.

## VATA/KAPHA – KAPHA/VATA

Vata/kapha is a combination of ether, air, water and earth. You should follow the kapha eating and living plan during the winter and spring months and in cold, damp weather, and follow the vata plan in the autumn and summer months, and during cold, dry windy spells.

The vata/kapha type is cold and can therefore have plenty of pungent, hot and spicy foods. Examples of suitable foods include artichokes, asparagus,

mustard greens, parsnips, summer and winter squashes and watercress. Vegetables with seeds should be well cooked with the appropriate vata spices to minimize aggravation. Fresh seasonal fruits can be eaten, including apricots, berries, cherries, lemons, mangoes, peaches and strawberries. The vata/kapha type should avoid a mono-diet of brown rice. Herbs and spices for this type include allspice, anise, asafoetida (hing), black pepper, cinnamon, cloves, curry powder, garlic, nutmeg, poppy seeds, saffron and vanilla.

## TRIDOSHA

In very rare instances a person may score more or less equally for all three doshas, revealing themselves to be all three types or "tridosha". If you are a combination of all three doshas you will require a tridoshic diet and living plan. Follow the seasonal changes and eat according to the

▶ Use cloves and cinnamon to flavour hot, spicy dishes and warming drinks.

weather or your personal circumstances. On hot days, and during the spring and summer months, follow the pitta plan; on cold days and during the winter months, follow the kapha plan, and during the late summer and autumn or on windy

▲ Vata/kapha – kapha/vata herbs and spices include asafoetida, allspice, curry powder, pepper-corns, curry leaves, nutmeg, cinnamon, cloves and vanilla pods.

days or cold dry weather follow the vata plan.

If you find that you fall into this unusual category, it is advisable to consult an Ayurvedic practitioner to find out more about tridosha.

# AYURVEDIC SELF-HELP IN THE HOME

Before you begin to read this section, or consider treating yourself for a complaint, note that it is *vitally important* that pregnant women, children, or anyone who has severe health problems, or uses prescription medicine, should consult an Ayurvedic physician or other doctor before using any Ayurvedic herbs or other treatments.

In Ayurvedic medicine you always treat a condition with its opposite. For a burn, for example, which is hot and dry, you would

▼ The gel from aloe vera can be used to treat minor burns.

administer something cool and moist, such as the gel from the leaves of an aloe vera plant. Ayurveda does not treat the condition, it treats the pattern of the body type. This means that there will be three different types

▲ Heat and steam is a remedy for certain kapha conditions as it acts as a powerful stimulus.

of treatment, according to whether the condition is vata, pitta or kapha in nature. Vata

▶ Tai chi is particularly therapeutic for the pitta dosha.

symptoms will be changeable, arising from tension and stress. They should be treated with relaxation, warmth and calm. Pitta conditions will be hot and intense, and are related to the liver, arising from suppressed anger or frustration. They should be treated with cool, relaxing things that help to release the suppressions. Kapha conditions will be dull and congestive.

Some conditions may be vata, pitta or kapha, according to the symptoms, while others are generally linked with one dosha. Diarrhoea, for example, is a pitta condition, and constipation is a vata one. When referring to the following information, you will

▼ Gentle yoga is suitable for vata people.

need to discover whether your condition is displaying vata, pitta or kapha symptoms. You can then turn to the relevant vata, pitta or kapha section and follow the outlined plan for treatment to reduce the excess in that

particular dosha, which is irritating the condition.

You should lessen the recommended treatments when symptoms subside, especially the Ayurvedic herbs or spices. However, if you are a particular doshic type with a condition from the same dosha, maintain the appropriate plan with moderate use of the herbs and spices. Remember that some conditions will require proper medical treatment. Diarrhoea, for example, can cause serious loss of body fluids and tissue salts, especially if vomiting is involved as well. Be sensible with your self-help regime and always consult a qualified Ayurvedic or medical doctor if your condition either worsens or fails to respond to the treatment.

# THE GASTRO-INTESTINAL TRACT

In Ayurvedic medicine, the gastro-intestinal tract (GI) is the most important part of the body, as it is thought to be the seat of the doshas. Vata is formed in the colon, pitta in the small intestine and kapha in the stomach.

## CONSTIPATION

Drink warm liquids; hot water is acceptable, but not chilled water. Herbs for constipation are triphala and satisabgol (psyllium husks). (Do not use triphala if

VATA AND THE GASTRO-INTESTINAL TRACT
Regular daily bowel movements are a sign of a healthy GI. Typical vata conditions of the GI include constipation, gas/flatulence, and tension – cramps or spasms, such as irritable bowel syndrome.

▲ Eating a healthy vata diet can aid many vata problems associated with the gastro-intestinal tract.

you are pregnant or suffering from ulcers of the GI.) Triphala is a combination of three herbal fruits, each of which has a rejuvenating effect in relation to one of the doshas. Satisabgol is a demulcent laxative. It is gentle and soothing and holds moisture in the colon, thus helping vata, which is dry and cold. Satisabgol can be used with triphala, as they complement one another.

## GAS, BLOATING, COLIC

These symptoms are usually related to constipation. Ideally food should pass through the system in 24 hours. If left for

much longer there is fermentation, which causes a build-up of gas. The herbal remedy for this is hingvastak, a mix of asafoetida, pippali, ginger, black pepper, cumin, wild celery seeds and rock salt.

A massage with brahmi oil – a medicated oil that is used to restore and relax the nervous system – is another traditional Ayurvedic remedy.

▼ When massaging, follow the direction of the colon – from lower left, across the abdomen, up to the right and across to the left.

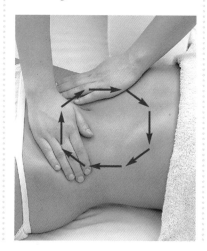

▲ Nettle tea is very good at balancing the digestive system and can help to alleviate pitta conditions such as diarrhoea.

## ACIDITY/HEARTBURN

Sip aloe vera juice (without any citric acid added). Add fresh and dried coriander (cilantro), turmeric, saffron, coconut, fennel or peppermint to your diet. Shatavari *(Asparagus racemosus),* licorice (not to be used with high blood pressure or oedema) and amalaki are used in Ayurveda to balance acidity.

## DIARRHOEA

Pitta diarrhoea is generally hot, and often yellowish and foul-smelling. Diarrhoea is mainly related to pitta but can sometimes be caused by other factors, such as high toxicity (ama), stress or emotional factors. Persistent symptoms must be dealt with by a physician.

If you have diarrhoea, avoid hot spices and follow the pitta plan. Eat abstemiously if at all, drinking plenty of fluids and adding coriander (cilantro), saffron and a little cardamom, fresh ginger and nutmeg to your diet. A simple diet of rice, split mung dhal and vegetables is most suitable for the pitta dosha, while symptoms last.

▼ Vegetables for the pitta diet.

## PITTA AND THE GASTRO-INTESTINAL TRACT

Pitta digestion tends to be fast and "burns" food. This is made worse by anger or frustration. Begin a pitta-reducing diet and eat in a calm and relaxed way. Typical pitta conditions of the gastro-intestinal tract include acidity and heartburn, symptomized by belching and acid indigestion; diarrhoea or frequent loose bowel movements, and constant hunger, accompanied by consequent irritability.

## PERSISTENT HUNGER/INCREASED APPETITE

In general, follow the pitta plan and use aloe vera juice as above. Increase relaxation, meditation and yoga. Have a massage with brahmi oil. If strong symptoms persist, consult your physician.

## KAPHA AND THE GASTRO-INTESTINAL TRACT

Typical kapha conditions of the GI include poor appetite – kapha tends to be low in *agni* (digestive fire), which can create a slow metabolism and weight gain; nausea; a build-up of mucus, leading to colds, sinus problems, coughs and flu; and poor circulation, resulting in a build-up of toxicity (ama). Follow the kapha plan and eat plenty of hot spices, such as chilli peppers, garlic, ginger and black pepper, until the condition clears, after which you should reduce your intake of hot spices. Herbs for kapha conditions of the GI include trikatu ("three hot things"), to be taken or added to meals. This contains pippali, ginger and black pepper. You should also have plenty of vigorous exercise.

## NAUSEA

Ginger and cardamom tea will often calm nausea. To make it, peel and thinly slice a piece of fresh ginger, add five cardamom pods and pour boiled spring water over them. Leave to stand for five minutes and drink while still hot.

Ginger is a carminative and a stimulant. This means that it has the ability to combat intestinal bloating and to speed processes in the GI so that balance is restored. During the winter and spring, when kapha is seasonally high, dried ginger can be blended with some boiled spring water and a little honey to help keep the digestive system active and moving, so helping to reduce the

▲ Hot kapha dietary spices.

risk of colds, coughs and flu.

Cardamom (common in Southern India as well as other tropical areas) can be used for kapha and vata digestive conditions, although only in small amounts as it can aggravate pitta or bring about a pitta excess. As with all the recommended foods, herbs and spices, the purer the quality, the more beneficial they will be. Therefore, try to buy organic herbs and spices when possible.

▶ Ginger root.

▼ Ginger and cardamom tea.

# COMMON PROBLEMS

The forms taken by commonly occurring illnesses and the appropriate remedies will vary according to whether you have a vata, pitta or kapha dosha.

### INSOMNIA

Any vata-increasing influence can contribute to insomnia, including lots of travel, stress, an irregular or ungrounded lifestyle and the use of stimulants such as tea and coffee. The herbs used to treat vata-based insomnia are brahmi (*Centella*), jatamansi, ashwagandha (*Withania somnifera*) and nutmeg. A massage using brahmi oil will be beneficial.

▼ A foot massage with brahmi oil will often relieve insomnia.

▲ Juice from aloe vera plants can be used to combat sleeplessness.

Insomnia in the pitta dosha is brought on by anger, jealousy, frustration, fever, excess sun or heat. Follow the pitta plan, which is cooling, and take brahmi, jatamansi, bhringaraj (*Eclipta alba*), shatavari and aloe vera juice. Massage brahmi oil into the head and feet.

As kapha types like to sleep and tend to be sleepy, they rarely suffer from insomnia.

### HEADACHE/MIGRAINE

Vata headaches cause extreme pain and are related to anxiety and tension. Treatments include

triphala to clear any congestion, jatamansi, brahmi and calamus.

Pitta headaches are associated with heat or burning sensations, flushed skin and visual sensitivity to light. They are related to anger, frustration or irritability, and will be connected to the liver and gall bladder. Treatments are brahmi, turmeric and aloe vera juice.

Kapha headaches are dull and heavy and can cause nausea. There may also be congestion, such as catarrh. Have a stimulating massage, with minimal oil, and take plenty of exercise to alleviate congestion.

▼ Massage the head with sandalwood, coconut or brahmi oil for pitta insomnia.

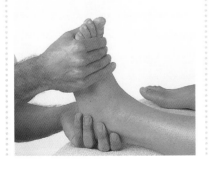

## COLDS

A tendency to mucus production or catarrh/phlegm is usually due to poor digestion of foods in the stomach which increases ama (toxicity) and kapha. In general, kapha is the main dosha involved.

Vata-type colds involve dry symptoms, such as a dry cough or dry throat. Herbs for vata coughs and colds are ginger, cumin, pippali, tulsi (holy basil, *Ocimum*

▼ Adding puréed spearmint leaves to a bowl of warm water makes a soothing footbath for pitta-type colds.

*sanctum*), cloves and peppermint, licorice (not to be used with high blood pressure or oedema), shatavari and ashwagandha. Put one or two drops of sesame oil up each nostril and follow the vata plan until symptoms subside.

Pitta-type colds involve more heat, the face is usually red and there may even be a fever. The mucus is often yellow and can contain blood. Herbs for pitta coughs and colds are peppermint and other mints, sandalwood, chrysanthemum and a little tulsi (holy basil). Follow the pitta plan until symptoms subside.

▲ Spiced hot lemon tea for kapha colds.

Kapha colds are thick and mucusy, with a feeling of heaviness in the head and/or body. Avoid cold, damp weather and exposure to cold and damp conditions. Eliminate sugar, refined foods, meat and nuts, dairy products, bread, fats and oils from the diet and use plenty of hot spices. Drink a spiced tea of hot lemon, ginger and cinnamon with cloves or tulsi, sweetened with a little raw honey. Herbs for kapha colds are ginger, cinnamon, pippali, tulsi (holy basil), cloves and peppermint. Saunas and hot baths will help to increase the heat of the kapha person, but they should not be used in excess as this would increase pitta too much. Follow the kapha plan until symptoms subside.

## COUGHS

Vata coughs are dry and irritated with very little mucus, the chief symptom being a painful cough often accompanied by a dry mouth. Herbs and spices for the vata cough include licorice (do not use this if you have high blood pressure or oedema), shatavari, ashwagandha and cardamom. Follow the vata plan until the symptoms subside.

▼ It is worth having a supply of fresh mint and other herbs to hand for many of the common Ayurvedic treatments.

Pitta coughs are usually associated with a lot of phlegm. The chest is congested, but the mucus cannot be brought up properly. There is often fever or heat, combined with a burning sensation in the chest or throat. High fevers should be treated by a physician, and people with asthma should consult their doctor immediately if a cough or cold leads to wheezing and difficult breathing. The best herbs for pitta coughs include peppermint, tulsi (holy basil) and sandalwood. Follow the pitta plan until the symptoms have completely subsided.

▲ Cardamom pods are beneficial to vata-type coughs.

With kapha coughs, the patient usually brings up lots of phlegm, and suffers a loss of appetite combined with nausea. The chest is loaded with mucus, but this may not be coughed up because the kapha individual is likely to feel tired. Treatments for kapha coughs are raw honey, lemon, cloves and chyawanprash (a herbal jam). Follow the kapha plan until the symptoms subside, increasing your intake of hot spices, and use trikatu powder. Keep warm and avoid damp, cold environments.

## SKIN PROBLEMS

These are often caused by internal conditions of toxicity (ama) and are mainly related to the pitta dosha.

Vata skin problems will be dry and rough. Avoid letting the skin dry out, and exposing it to cold and/or windy weather. Herbal remedies for vata skin are triphala and satisabgol (the latter is also useful if you are constipated).

Pitta skin problems will be red, swollen, raised or inflamed, often with a yellow head or yellow pus discharge. Avoid sun, heat or hot baths, and increase your intake of salads, raw vegetables and fruits.

Follow the pitta plan and add turmeric, coriander and saffron to your diet. The remedies for pitta skin problems are manjishta (*Rubia cordifolia*), kutki (*Picrohiza kurroa*), neem (*Azadirachta indica*), turmeric and aloe vera juice.

Kapha skin problems will involve congestion in the blood, which can cause the skin to form thick and mucusy whiteheads. Increase your level of exercise, and follow the kapha plan. Treatments for kapha skin conditions include a small amount of calamus, cinnamon, cloves, dry ginger, trikatu formula and turmeric.

▲ Fresh fruit is suitable for pitta skin conditions.

◀ Fresh figs are among the fruits recommended for the vata diet.

▼ Cloves for kapha conditions.

## URINARY INFECTIONS

The kidneys are very important in Ayurvedic medicine. In the West, we tend to overburden our kidneys by the use of diuretics. In Ayurveda the body is considered to be chiefly made up of plasma rather than water. Excess cold water, tea, coffee, and alcoholic drinks will weaken the kidneys. Salt, sugar or foods that are rich in calcium, such as dairy products or spinach, will similarly tend to weaken and toxify the kidneys. The best kidney tonic to use in Ayurveda is shilajit, a mineral-rich compound from the Himalayan mountains, but this should be avoided if you suffer from kidney stones.

▼ Add cinnamon to your diet to relieve kapha-type cystitis.

▲ Lime and coconut are recommended for pitta cystitis.

Pregnant women, children or those on medication should consult an Ayurvedic practitioner before treatment.

## CYSTITIS

In vata people, cystitis will tend to be less intense. Remedies are shilajit (to be avoided if you suffer from kidney stones) with bala (*Sida cordifolia*), ashwagandha and shatavari.

Cystitis is mainly a pitta condition because it burns and is hot and inflamed. Follow the pitta plan, using plenty of coriander (cilantro) and avoiding hot food and spices. Remedies are aloe vera juice (not to be used in pregnancy), lime juice, coconut, coriander, pomegranate, punarnava (*Boerrhaavia diffusa*), shilajit and sandalwood.

Kapha-type cystitis is accompanied by congestion and mucus in the urinary tract, and the urine is often pale or clear. The treatments are cinnamon, trikatu combined with shilajit, gokshura (*Tribulis terrestris*) and gokshurdi guggul.

# ADDRESSES, SUPPLIERS & ACKNOWLEDGEMENTS

UK ADDRESSES
Almadel Natural Health Centre
PO Box 2453, Frome
Somerset BA11 3YH
Tel: 01373 812864
Courses and consultations run by
Sally Morningstar.

The Ayurvedic Trading Company
The Old Clinic
10 St John's Square, Glastonbury
Somerset BA6 9LJ
Tel: 01458 833382
Ayurvedic herbs and spices.

The Yoga for Health Foundation
Ickwell, Bury
Biggleswade SG18 9EB
Tel: 01767 627271
Courses in yoga and Ayurveda.

US ADDRESSES
The Ayurvedic Institute
P.O. Box 23445
Albuquerque, NM 87192-1445
Tel: (505) 291 9698
Fax: (505) 294 7572

The Ayurvedic Center
7751 San Felipe, Suite 200
Houston, TX 77063
Tel: (713) 785 4474

EverGreen Herb Garden and
Learning Center
PO Box 1445
Placerville, CA 95667
Tel: (530) 626 9288

Bioveda
215 North Route 303
Congers, NY 10920-1726
Tel: (800) 292 6002
www.adh-heath.com
Sells Ayurvedic herbs and products.

SEEKING PROFESSIONAL HELP
To find an Ayurvedic doctor who
will be able to go into detail about
treatments for your condition, a
register of qualified practitioners is
available from the Ayurvedic Medical
Association, 59 Dulverton Road,
Selsdon, Croydon, Surrey CR2 8PJ.
Tel: 0181 657 6147

PICTURE ACKNOWLEDGEMENTS
The publishers would like to thank
the following agencies for permission
to reproduce their images:
**Edimedia:** 15l
**E.T. Archive:** 9r and 10l
**Images:** The Charles Walker
Collection: 14r
**Tony Stone Images:** 8, 10r, 14l,
16l, 17r, 18, 19r, 25, 35 and 43
**Key:** l = left, r = right

AUTHOR'S ACKNOWLEDGEMENTS
My thanks to Andrew Johnson from
the Ayurvedic Trading Company for
his invaluable professional guidance,
to Collette Prideux Brune,
aromatherapist, to Sarah Duffin at
Anness Publishing for her unfailing
persistence with a very complex
subject, and my deepest thanks to the
divine will of God – for everything!